Thoughts from the Cradle

A Christian physician's reflections during
two tours in Iraq

Kirk A. Milhoan, MD, PhD

PRESS

7/6/17

Dear Bully,

I pray that my thoughts
are a blessing to your heart
soul.

Soli Deo Gloria

2 TIM 1:7

Dedication

To all who are willing to give their lives so that others may be free.

Acknowledgement

First and foremost, I am eternally indebted to my Lord and Savior, Jesus Christ, whose Spirit and Word guided me as I wrote these thoughts. Secondly, LTC Mark Murphy, who was my friend during my first tour and was a constant encouragement to continue to share my thoughts. Thirdly, my dear friend since junior high school, Tim Rogers, who was gracious enough to post these thoughts on his website. Finally, my family: my son Drew, who was forced to share his father with those helping Iraq to become free; my mother Judy, who was a tireless encouragement to me in word, e-mail, care packages and, most importantly, prayers; and the lovely Dr. Kimberly Milhoan, my wife, my best friend. The thought of seeing her beautiful face and holding her in my arms one more time kept me going through some of the darkest days of my life.

Introduction

During my two tours in Iraq, I had a desire to share my thoughts. These are my personal musings inspired by my relationship with my Savior Jesus Christ and reading His word, and my life as a husband, father, son, physician and Air Force officer. I thank God for the grace He extended me while I was in Iraq to experience the best and worst of man. "Thoughts from the Cradle" are my impressions of my experiences in Iraq. Why "the Cradle"? Iraq has been called the cradle of civilization since the Tigris and Euphrates Rivers meet in Southern Iraq. The book of Genesis states that the Garden of Eden was located near the joining of theses two rivers. As a person who believes in the inerrancy of the Bible, I believe that Adam and Eve first lived in what is now called Iraq. I do not believe that the account in Genesis is a metaphor. There is some question over the exact location of the Garden of Eden since there is also a location in Turkey where the Tigris and Euphrates meet. However, since Abraham was a Chaldean from Ur, modern day Kuwait and Southern Iraq, I am inclined to believe that Iraq is the true location of the literal Garden of Eden.

APRIL 28, 2005

It's very strange to be talking to your best friend as he gets ready to head off to Iraq within the next 14 hours. Fortunately, he's pretty excited to be serving his country. He will also, hopefully, be using this blog to record his thoughts of his 4-month tour. His handle is "Duke" and I ask for prayers for him but also his wife and son.

His departing thoughts are best summed up by the US Armed Forces Code of Conduct, specifically Article 6, which states:

I will never forget that I am an American, fighting for freedom, responsible for my actions and dedicated to the principles that made my country free. I will trust in my God and in the United States of America.

Tim Rogers

www.Brokenmasterpieces.com

APRIL 29, 2005

Goodbye

I said goodbye to my wife and son today. This was a different goodbye. Mostly, because there is a very real sense that this could be the last goodbye with the next hello occurring in heaven. It was also very emotional to see all the other families saying goodbye to their loved ones. One specific family was a single mother of five boys who was leaving her children in the care of their grandparents. It was very difficult for the boys. They were struggling to see who got to sit on Mom's lap. As I looked around the auditorium where we said our last good-byes, I was reminded of what a sacrifice the 100+ thousand deployed troops have made for the US, Iraq, and the world. Many of these same soldiers, airmen, Marines, and seamen qualify for governmental assistance to feed their families. I am proud to say I serve with these fine fighting folks. I am not going to fight. That is not my role. I am going to medically support the soldiers and the flyers and to help bring them home alive. I especially want to see the mother of five young boys come home.

Soli Deo Gloria

More thoughts to come

MAY 5, 2005

Arriving

As we flew into Iraq airspace, we flew over Mosul, which is the ancient city of Nineveh. This is the city that Jonah was asked to go and speak to in **Jonah 1:2 : "Arise, go to Nineveh the great city and cry against it, for** their wickedness has come up before Me." As the story goes, Jonah refused to follow God's direction and tried to escape by boat. A storm came and he admitted that it was his fault and the crew should throw him overboard. They threw him overboard and the sea calmed. Jonah was swallowed by a whale (there are verified accounts of men being swallowed by at least two whales, as well as one dog, and surviving). When he realized his true mistake, he called out to God. This one statement is quite profound: "**Those who cling to worthless idols forfeit the grace that could be theirs (Jonah 2:8).**" (New International Version) He was then spit out on the beach and he went to Nineveh. I think we often make our own comforts an idol. We do not do what God is calling us to do because we may have to give up those comforts. I was given this quote from my father-in law who is one of my heroes. He served in the Air Force and won the Distinguished Flying Cross for his service in Viet Nam. I think it applies very well to the current attitude that many hold in the US.

"War is an ugly thing, but not the ugliest of things. The decayed and degraded state of moral and patriotic feelings which thinks that nothing is worth war is much worse. The person who has nothing for which he is willing to fight, nothing which is more important than his own personal safety, is a miserable creature and has no chance of being free unless made and kept so by the exertions of better men than himself." - John Stewart Mill

13

I think this quote exemplifies how our selfishness and desire to protect ourselves can many times prevent us from achieving a higher good. I believe God is always looking for us to have absolute dependence on Him even if that takes us into harm's way. As it says in **Philippians 1:21 "For to me, to live is Christ and to die is gain."**

I wonder in my own life how many times God has called me to do something and, just like Jonah, I ran from the task, only to find myself in an even worse predicament.

Soli Deo Gloria

More thoughts to come

MAY 6, 2005

Blood Run

I had a very interesting day today. I was able to fly with an air evacuation helicopter. The helicopter was a Blackhawk, specifically configured to fly the injured.

The first flight was a blood run. That is to take blood to bases that are in urgent need. On this trip we had three stops. The first stop was the major army hospital in Baghdad. the next was Baghdad International Airport, and the third was Abu Ghraib Prison. Yes, that is the same prison that was in the news so much.

As we flew low and fast across Iraq, I was impressed once again of the life that water brings. I first saw this when I was traveling to Sudan and was flying over the Nile. Within a quarter-mile of the river, there was vegetation and everything was lush. Past that it was desert and it appeared that there was nothing alive. It reminded me of what Jesus said, **"He who believes in me, as the Scripture said, 'From his inner most being will flow living water' (John 7:38)"**. The river we were flying over in Iraq was the Euphrates. It is still hard for me to believe that I am here and what I am seeing. Along the Euphrates there was vegetation everywhere. I was also impressed at the number of date palms. There were literally thousands of them and many orchards. Every house seemed to have its own date palm. I can see why Dates play such an important role in their recipes.

The thought that came to mind when we were landing at Abu Ghraib was from **Matthew 5:43 "You have heard that it was said, 'You shall love your neighbor and hate your enemy.' But I say to you: Love your enemies and pray for those who persecute you."** Many have said that giving blood is the gift of life. Over here when there is a call for blood, in minutes there will be a response from the troops. They realize that it may be one of their friends who needs blood or someday it may be their life that will be saved by the blood of another. When the troops give blood, they have no idea when and where it will be used. But they give out of a desire to help and care for others. During war blood is precious. Giving such a precious gift to an enemy to help save his life is a great example of living out this verse. Some of the patients who have received blood are same ones who, when they are on the medical ward, try to urinate on the techs and the nurses as they care for them. That reminds me of what Jesus said on the cross: **"Father, forgive them, for they do not know not what they doing (Luke 23:34)."**

There are many difficult situations here and I am very grateful that I have Jesus' life to be an example, and the help of the Holy Spirit to live it out.

Soli Deo Gloria

More thoughts to come

MAY 11, 2005

Medical Air Evacuation ("Aerovac")

I wanted to share some of what is involved to get injured service members back home. When someone is injured they are evaluated to see what type of care they may need. Those appropriate are treated and stay with their units. Those who need more sophisticated care come to one of the theater hospitals and then are either sent back to their unit after recovering or are sent forward to a hospital in Germany and then eventually home. This whole process can take less than 36 hours to get a patient from the battle to the plane going to Germany.

The other night, I was clearing soldiers to travel to Germany. There were more patients than usual due to the recent offensive in Northern Iraq along the Syrian border. I would ask each man how they were injured. They were very willing to tell their story as long as they were not in too much pain. Most of the guys had their arms and/or legs injured. There was a tank crew that ran over a double stacked mine that blew up the inside of the tank. The three guys inside all had varied injuries. One the guys had both legs and his arm injured. His buddy realized that he was injured and started pulling him out of the tank. He then realized that his leg and arm were injured and was able to help pull his buddy out using one leg and one arm. There were many stories like this. These two men were stabilized at the theater hospital and were now on their way to Germany. They were on litters and receiving significant pain meds. There were also many who had wounds that needed more care but they were able to walk.

When the plane arrives we take the wounded warriors to the plane. We load the litter patients first. There are many soldiers who volunteer from various units and come to help the medics. They consider this an honor to help their fellow soldiers. The litters are stacked three high tonight. There will be close to 40 patients going on the plane, 22 on litters. There will also be two patients on ventilators.

We load the most serious of the litter patients last. One soldier has external fixators holding both his legs together. I touch his shoulder as I say, "have a safe trip home." It brings tears to my eyes. This warrior has given much for his country. It is truly an honor to care for him.

Next we load the walking patients. As the bus pulls up, all the people who were involved in loading the litter patients form a tunnel, much like what cheerleaders may do at a sporting event. However, this is much more somber. The people forming the tunnel applaud as the walking wounded board the bus with well wishes of: "have a safe trip," "thanks for all you did," "they'll take good care of you in Germany," and "God bless you."

The team of medics have been working non-stop since receiving these patients earlier in the evening to get the patients out tonight. The plane now closes its cargo doors. It's 0430. This will undoubtedly repeat tomorrow until there is peace and freedom in Iraq.

Soli Deo Gloria

More thoughts to come

MAY 13, 2005

The Crucible

The other day I had the opportunity to be a part of a medevac helicopter mission. There was an injured patient who was an urgent transport (typically these patients are on a ventilator and in need of more advanced care than can be provided where they are). When the helicopter crew heard of the mission all they knew was that an urgent patient needed to be transported from Tikrit to Balad. Tikrit has the ability to do some surgery, but for more complicated cases they need to go to Balad. Shortly after we landed at Sadaam's hometown, another helicopter landed. This was going to be a tail-to-tail transfer, meaning the patient does not stop at the hospital. The team unloaded the patient from the other helicopter and loaded him onto our helicopter. It became obvious that this was an Iraqi, or at least appeared to be. He had been shot in the neck and was going to be a quadriplegic. He was on a transport ventilator, which was breathing for him. There was also a monitor that showed a continuous read-out of his pulse and blood pressure. I was monitoring his vital signs as we finished loading the helo. All of his values were borderline. The critical care nurse then boarded and took over the monitoring. During the flight his blood pressure dropped and he required a significant increase in his medications to keep his blood pressure at low normal values. When this occurred the pilots, always cognizant of the condition of the patients they are carrying, pushed the nose of the helicopter over to increase the speed. We arrived just minutes later at the hospital in Balad. There was a team waiting for us that quickly took the patient to the ICU.

When I told the stories to others, I was asked whether he was a good guy or a bad guy. At that point I realized that I hadn't considered that when I was transporting him. I was glad that I was able to focus on my role and not allow the side he was fighting on to change the way I would care for him. This is probably one of the most difficult issues for doctors over here. They may routinely have the villain and the innocent in the same ICU. It is probably for the best that most of the time we do not know who is on which side.

Many may ask what are we doing taking care of the enemy. My response would come from a parable that Jesus taught us. In Luke 10: 25-37, Jesus tells a story of when a Jew had been robbed and beaten. A priest and a Levite pass him and do nothing to help. Then a man from Samaria, hated by the Jews, stops and cares for him and then makes arrangements for his continuing care. Jesus exalts this man as one who truly showed love for his neighbor.

So what about us medics in the armed forces taking care of these guys who are trying to kill us? We give them our blood and the best medical care that can be found in Iraq. What would they probably do if we were injured? Well, if history is our guide, they may drag us through the streets. I think that type of behavior would qualify them as the very least of our brethren. **In Matthew 25: 40 Jesus states "Truly I say to you, to the extent that you did it to one of these brothers of Mine, even the least of them, you did it to me."**

The time in Iraq is a crucible for my faith and I need God's gift of compassion and grace and mercy more than ever.

Soli Deo Gloria

More thoughts to come

MAY 16, 2005

Patriot Detail

I was a part of a Patriot Detail the other day. That is when service members send off a fallen comrade. Today it was for an army specialist who died during recent operations.

I will include a wonderful description of the Patriot Detail that has previously been written. What I wanted to share were the thoughts that were going through my mind as we gathered for this solemn event.

As we fell into formation, soldiers from the specialist's unit came to lead the formation. Just seeing them brought tears to my eyes. I could not imagine how hard it must be to say good-bye to a friend in this way. The chaplain's vehicle drove past our formation. Next, I caught site of a Humvee carrying the flag-draped casket. The U.S. flag is so beautiful. Covering a casket, it takes on a sobering and sacred hue. We were called to attention and then ordered to march as we lead the procession to the plane that would carry this fallen hero home. Eight army soldiers were on point. We came to the plane, stopped and then faced in. We were called to present arms, a very slow salute to be held until the hero was on the plane. Four friends from his unit carried the casket. The casket was loaded on the plane and we slowly lowered our salute. The formation then entered the aircraft to hear the final words from the chaplain. You could hear sniffles, the audible evidence of tears. My thoughts went to his family. They were waiting for their loved one to come home ever since they had received that visit from the official vehicle that no family wants to see in their driveway when a loved one is deployed. This reunion was not going to be the one they had dreamed about and longed for. No, this is the one they had hoped and prayed would never happen. The family was hours away from receiving their loved one, under a flag.

My thoughts then went to my own family. What would it be like for them if I returned under a flag? What would it be like for my son, my wife, and my mom to wait at an airport for me to come off a plane? To come off not waving with smiles, running for the touch of my most loved; but, rather, carried off in a solemn processional. The emotions are very difficult to suppress. I cry even as I type this. It was harder when the casket was before me.

What a burden that this family is now carrying. My thoughts go to the comforting words of Jesus. "Come to me all those who are heavy laden." I hope that this family will find the peace that only Christ can give.

Soli Deo Gloria

More thoughts to come

Patriot Detail

Iraq — Somewhere in America a family member is waiting for their relative to return home. He is returning early, having served his profession with pride and excellence.

We won't be there to honor his arrival, but we were there when more than 100 of his fellow professionals saw him off with respect and dignity. His title, and the title of thousands of his like-minded brothers and sisters, is specialist. For their profession is to defend the United States of America.

The Soldiers of his unit and the Airmen of our 332nd Expeditionary Wing stood at attention, in a cordon of desert camouflage uniforms, as six of his unit's young men stood ready to carry their brother to his place on the start of his journey home. Just before they begin their solemn march, we are ordered to present arms, and for three seconds our right arms were slowly raised to touch the corner of our eyes. As the detail passed we held our salute, honoring our comrade in arms and the Stars and Stripes as they pass by. We held our salute until he was secured in his place of honor, then after the first sergeant's command, we slowly brought our arms to our side.

Still at attention, with eyes straight ahead, I could observe several faces with trails of tears, men and women alike, young and old, for we had lost one of our own, one who put service before self.

Next the Army chaplain marched between our columns to join his troop on the plane. Only then were we released from formation, but told we may march onto the plane for the Chaplain's comments. No one walked away. Every member of the formation joined together, side by side, until there was no room to stand inside the plane. But the others stood respectfully just outside the plane's rear entrance, as the chaplain recited the 23rd Psalm before he said a prayer for our departing brother and his family.

Slowly we left the plane so the specialist could begin the journey home. As I looked back into the cargo bay, I saw something I will never forget. Members of his unit saluted the flag on their own; some touched it respectfully. One soldier leaned over and put his forehead briefly next to the stars, as if putting his forehead on his brother's forehead.

As our Air Force members slowly left the area, the Army again fell into formation. They stood at attention as the plane rolled away.

Yes, somewhere someone is waiting for their loved one's final journey home. We wish he hadn't left early. We gave him a final salute with heartfelt pride and professional excellence. His sacrifice to duty, honor, and country demanded we offer no less. We are the profession of arms. All of us made a commitment to serve. Most of us made some sacrifice while in service. Some made the ultimate sacrifice.

MAY 18, 2005

An Artificial Lung

I am flying over Romania in a C-141 on my way back to Iraq. I went to Germany to help care for a critical patient who was being aerovac'd to Landstuhl Regional Medical Center. This Marine was injured in an IED (improvised explosive device) blast. His lungs had been injured and he was placed on a new device that acts like an artificial lung. This patient had multiple injuries and was on a ventilator, with 4 chest tubes and was what we like to say "4+ sick". We were not sure whether he would tolerate the airplane ride.

The reason that two doctors came from Germany to place the device was that his lungs were so damaged that he would decompensate every time that he was moved in his bed. The hope was that this device would enable him to stabilize to the point where we could move him; if not, he would probably die in Iraq. So, how many people were involved in this one soldier's care? It starts with the medic on the ground. Then the medic flying on the Blackhawk helicopter, which also has two pilots and a crew chief, took over. The soldier was then taken to Balad, where there was a team who met the helicopter at the hospital. He was then taken emergently to surgery where an anesthesiologist made sure he was properly anesthetized and kept stable for surgery. The surgeon operated with the help of a nurse and a scrub tech. The Marine was then transferred to the ICU where he had multiple physicians, techs and nurses caring for him. When he wasn't doing very well two physicians flew in from Germany to attempt placing the new device. He then had another trip to the OR for the device placement and getting his wounds further cleaned out. Then he went back to the ICU. He had a rocky course after the device was placed which required consultation with surgeons, a cardiologist and even a pediatric cardiologist. The pediatric cardiologist was called because this device mimics the physiology of lesions that children with complex heart disease may have.

After 4 days it was decided that it was time to try to get him to Germany. Now the Critical Care Air Transport Team (CCATT) team was mobilized. This team is composed of a critical care physician, a critical care nurse and a respiratory therapist. I went along as a flight surgeon to help if he deteriorated in flight, as did the cardiothoracic surgeon that placed the device.

The team to move the patient from the hospital to the plane was quite impressive. It was necessary because of all the equipment that was required to keep this brave Marine alive. At one point going on to the plane there were at least ten people around this one litter, either holding the litter or holding equipment attached to the Marine. A crew of 7 who helped transfer the patient met the plane. When we arrived at the ICU there were at least 8 nurses, docs and techs waiting to provide care in the ICU. The transfer to Germany was successful and now he is recovering in a much better equipped ICU, with a lot less dust than in Ballad.

So why did I tell this story? Well, I think it illustrates a point that is at the very nature of God and how He cares for each of us as an individual.

All of this effort was made for one man. People may say what a waste of resources. Not in the military. Everyone who serves knows that the medics will do whatever it takes to get them home. We are not always successful, but you can trust that everything that can be done will be done. I am reminded of the conversation that Abraham had with God when God told him that he was going to destroy Sodom in Genesis 18. Abraham tried to figure out how many righteous people needed to be in the city for it to be saved. Abraham started at fifty and made it down to ten people. Abraham never asked any number lower than ten. I imagine that at that point he realized how compassionate and just God was. Jesus also demonstrated this principle as He would purposely go out of his way to minister to a single person. I completely believe in this principle of the worth of a single person.

Lastly, I wanted to share another story that happened a couple of years ago. There were two soldiers in a South American country that had a car accident and ended up in a local hospital that was poorly equipped to care for their urgent medical needs. This information got back to the command in the states and an aircraft was scrambled to go pick them up. One of the patients was on a ventilator. The other had very serious injuries but was awake. The awake soldier saw all of these soldiers coming into the hospital. His thought at the time was, "Wow, whoever these people are coming to get must be very important, to come all this way." At that instant the Colonel leading the team came up to the soldier and said, "Son, we are here to take you home."

Soli Deo Gloria

More thoughts to come

MAY 22, 2005

Why Not Me?

Before I left for Iraq, I asked a flight surgeon who was recently deployed, "what was the toughest part of the job?". She said, "I was not prepared for flying home on an airplane carrying flag-draped caskets." I could sense from her that it was that lingering question "why them and not me?" that caused her discomfort.

This is a question and an emotion that is very common here. Whether it is a death or just an injury, the question lingers and begs to be answered. The soldier who trades seats with his buddy and the buddy dies and he does not. The soldier who bends down into the protection of the turret just before the explosion. I heard these two stories in the last couple of days.

I believe the underlying issue is the permissive will of God. Why does God allow what He does? Why does it seem like God gives some people hints to change seats in a Humvee and others hear nothing? Some Christians have miraculous escapes from death and other Christians die tragically. The same can be said of non-Christians.

I do not pretend to understand the permissive will of God. I do not believe that I should. I thought of this while I was reading Exodus. (Being in the Middle East brings the book of Exodus to life.) In Exodus 21: 12-13 it states **"He who strikes a man so that he dies shall surely be put to death. But, if he lies in wait for him, but God lets him fall into his hand, then I will appoint you a place to which he may flee."** Another verse is Exodus 4:11: **" The Lord said to him, 'Who has made man's mouth? Or who has makes him mute or deaf, or seeing or blind? Is it not I the Lord?'"** Both of these verses show the control God has over both death and illness or disability.

Of course, volumes could be written on this subject, but briefly how do I reconcile the concept of an all-loving, all-powerful, and all-knowing God allowing death and suffering? My answer: I absolutely believe that God is good. If at any point there is a situation where this does not appear to be true, I accept that I probably do not have all the information, especially the future results of the permissive will of God. The disciples in John indirectly raised this question 9:2-3: "**And His disciples asked Him, 'Rabbi who sinned, this man or his parents, that he would be born blind?' 'It was neither that this man sinned nor his parents sinned; but it was so that the works of God might be displayed in him.'**"

I believe God is working in all of us to either bring us into right relationship with Him or refine the impurities out of us.

Job said it best after he lost almost everything, including his children: "**Naked I came from my mother's womb, and naked I shall return there. The Lord gave and the Lord has taken away; blessed be the name of the Lord (Job 1:21).**"

Soli Deo Gloria

More thoughts to come

MAY 22, 2005

Vengeance or Forgiveness

Talking with people who have been shot at or had vehicles or devices explode near them, I have seen a variety of emotions. Most have a quiet resolve. "This is the nature of the conflict and someone got to me before I got to them". I have seen others that hold deep resentment not only of the insurgents but also of the Iraqi people for not stopping the insurgency. In a few others I have seen a peace that seems to harbor no resentment at all. The latter reminds me of Joseph. Genesis contains the details of how Joseph was betrayed by his brothers. He ended up as a servant to an Egyptian master due to betrayal and then in jail as a result of a lie. He eventually was able to save his family from sure death from famine due to the position of honor God had eventually given him in Egypt.

When the family was finally reunited the brothers were very concerned at the revenge that Joseph might have in mind. Genesis 50:19-21 contains Josephs's response to his brothers who were begging for mercy and declaring they were his slaves: "But Joseph said to them, **'Do not be afraid, for am I in God's place? As for you, you meant evil against me, but God meant it for good in order to bring about this present result, to preserve many people alive. So therefore do not be afraid. I will provide for you and your little ones.' So he comforted them and spoke kindly to them."**

What an example of not only forgiveness but also a willingness to bless those who had persecuted him. The forgiveness of Joseph is a foretaste of the forgiveness of Christ. While he was being tormented on the cross he was able to say "Forgive them for they know not what they do."

Honestly, I have a long way to go in the forgiveness department. When I see our wounded soldiers and the innocent men, women and children of Iraq killed or wounded, I want vengeance. Once again the Bible is there to guide me. Romans 12:19-20 says **"Never take your own revenge, beloved, but leave room for the wrath of God, for it is written: 'Vengeance is Mine, I will repay', says the Lord. But if your enemy is hungry, feed him; and if he is thirsty give him a drink; for in so doing you will heap burning coals on his head."** I hope we as medics are doing this as we treat those who have attacked our soldiers.

Soli Deo Gloria

More thoughts to come

MAY 27, 2005

Memorial Day

The *Stars and Stripes* headline on May 25, 2005 was "Explosion, attacks kill 8 U.S. troops in Iraq- Deaths bring to 13 the number of American lives lost since Sunday."

As this is Memorial Day, my thoughts went
to all of those for whom Memorial Day
holds a special sadness: a second funeral
day. The loved ones of the men and women
whose memory is celebrated on this solemn
day do not consider this just another day
off, the beginning of the BBQ season, or the
preordained time when women can wear white
shoes. This is a day where they are forced to
face their loss once more.

What is there to say to those who still grieve?
There is a letter that is read during the movie
"Saving Private Ryan" that I feel is most
appropriate.

"Dear Madame,

I have been shown in the files of the War
Department a statement from the Adjuvant
General of Massachusetts, that you are the
mother of five sons who have died gloriously
on the field of battle. I feel how weak and
fruitless must be any words of mine that would
attempt to beguile you from the grief of a
loss so overwhelming. I cannot refrain from
tendering to you the consolation that may be
found in the thanks of the Republic they died
to save. I pray that our Heavenly Father may
assuage the anguish of your bereavement and
leave you only the cherished memory of the
loved and lost and the solemn pride that must
be yours to have laid so costly a sacrifice upon
the altar of freedom.

Yours very sincerely and respectfully,

Abraham Lincoln"

My sincere thanks and prayers are with those who are saddened by Memorial Day. Let us all remember the sacrifice of those we celebrate today.

Soli Deo Gloria

More thoughts to come

MAY 31, 2005

Honoring the fallen

It is the day after Memorial Day, which was a very meaningful day here. Memorial Day had a new relevance here because we have all seen fighting men who are now honored by this hallowed day.

I saw something interesting as I went to eat lunch at the dining facility #2., commonly referred to as "DFAC2". I have noticed for some time that there seems to be more people saying grace before they it eat here than what I see at home. I also see many more people crossing themselves before eating. I attribute it to the old adage "There aren't any atheists in fox holes." Some could think of this place as one large foxhole as no one knows where the next mortar or rocket that is lobbed over the wire may hit. But back to what I saw interesting. Since we are nine hours ahead we often see the news on the TV from what we would call yesterday. So as I ate lunch the news that we were watching was from the evening of Memorial Day. I am not sure what channel it was but it sounded like Ted Koppel, so I guess Nightline and ABC. The entire show was a memorial to all those that had died during this war. There were two faces on the screen at all times and Koppel announced each name. If this was done to honor these brave military members, I am all for it. However, if there were some political agenda to use this to decrease support for the effort in Iraq, then I think it is reprehensible. But again, I digress. The DFAC2 is usually a loud and raucous room. There are loud voices and laughter. Not today. The attitude was somber as people who would normally ignore the TV were drawn to the screen. People would stop as they were walking to their seats or as they left to spend some time looking at the screen. Not to look or to talk too loudly seemed disrespectful. I do not think many liked having the pictures showed to us. I think for many it brought back memories that were difficult to suppress and this tore off the scab of a partially healed wound. It brought back to mind the mortality of us all, including some friends that were now evidence of the finality of death.

I would like to think that all of these being honored were in heaven enjoying paradise with Jesus. I do not know if that is the case. Jesus' grace for forgiveness is free but according to the Bible it is still something that needs to be received by faith. **Romans 3:22-23 says "even the righteousness of God through faith in Jesus Christ for all who believe. There is no** distinction, for all have sinned and fall short of the glory of God, being justified as a gift by His grace through the redemption which is in Christ Jesus."

I hope that all of the faces that were shown on the TV had a saving faith. I hope that my time here may be as a witness to others of the love and the peace and the eternal security that comes through Christ Jesus alone. I hope to be a witness that never has to use words. The Israelites knew Moses had seen God because his face was radiant (Exodus 34:29.) I pray that God makes my face radiant.

Soli Deo Gloria

More thoughts to come

JUNE 1, 2005

Do not be anxious

We had a patient come through for evacuation because he was a danger to himself. He was a part of the convoys that are the constant target of improvised explosive devices (IEDs). He had seen at least three buddies injured from IEDs and he didn't want to go back home in pieces. He said he would rather end his own life than to be blown up. It seemed like this fighting man didn't feel anything or anyone was protecting him from harm.

My thoughts went to Hebrews 13:5-6 where it says "I will never desert you, nor will I ever forsake you. So that we say confidently, 'The

Lord is my Helper; I will not be afraid. What will man do to me?;"

It also reminded me a story I read in "Jesus Freaks," a book about Christian martyrs. The martyr was Thomas Hauker in England in the year 1555.

"Thomas." His friend lowered his voice so as not to be heard by the guard. "I have to ask you a favor. I need to know if what others say about the grace of God is true. Tomorrow, when they burn you at the stake, if the pain is tolerable and your mind is still at peace, lift your hands above your head. Do it right before you die. Thomas, I have to know."

Thomas Hauker whispered to his friend, "I will."

The next morning, Hauker was bound to the stake and the fire was lit. The fire burned a long time, but Hauker remained motionless. His skin was burnt to a crisp and his fingers were gone. Everyone watching supposed that he was dead.

Suddenly, miraculously, Hauker lifted his hands, still on fire, above his head. He reached them up to the living God, and then, with great rejoicing, clapped them together three times.

The people there broke into shouts of praise and applause. Hauker's friend had his answer.

Hauker lived out the verse in **Philippians 4:6-7** " Be anxious for nothing, but in everything, by prayer and supplications, with thanksgiving let your requests be made known to God. And the peace of God, which surpasses all comprehension, will guard your hearts and your minds in Christ Jesus."

Soli Deo Gloria

More thoughts to come

JUNE 2, 2005

Alarm Red

The alarm red signifies that we are under attack. When we hear the alarm red siren, we must seek shelter and don a helmet and body armor. We have had around 20 of these events in the past month. So far no personnel have been harmed during this rotation but in the past there have been injuries. Sometimes you can hear when the mortar hits and other times you can't. The base is very large and sometimes the mortars or rockets do not make it all the way to the base and fall short in the surrounding field. Sometimes you feel the concussion move through your body and other times it just sounds like someone slammed a door.

There are also days when the explosive experts set off the explosive devices or bombs that have been discovered. They let us know when these are going to occur by email. If you don't check your email, it is often impossible to tell what is a controlled detonation and what is a rocket or mortar attack.

What I have noticed in others and myself
is that when a door slams or a loud sound
is heard, everyone stops and looks around.
A whistling sound will have people looking
skyward. You can imagine how many everyday
sounds can alert those of us who have been
conditioned by 20 alarm reds.

A couple of months before I came to Iraq, I was
in a mother's room who just delivered a baby
with significant heart defect. I was explaining
what needed to be done for the baby in the
next couple of days in order for the infant to
survive. It was about 0500 and the father was
asleep in the chair. There was a classic Texas
thunderstorm occurring outside the window.
While I was talking with the mother a loud
thunderclap went through the room. The soldier
who was previously asleep jumped up from the
chair, eyes wide open. He looked around dazed,
like he was not sure where he was. His wife
spoke with great compassion as she said, "He
just got back from Iraq."

After only a month in Iraq I now know how
he felt. I wonder how long it will be after I
get home that a closing door or a car backfire
doesn't send me to thoughts of mortars and
rockets.

This is a very unnatural business we are
engaged in. I can see why people who have
been in combat are never quite the same after
they come home and why people who have
not been there can never really understand.
There are many different reactions to the alarm

reds. Some cry and others find them annoying. Some never take off their body armor. Some will not put it on unless ordered to do so. I do not worry much about the mortar attacks and I think that is because I feel God's will will be done whether I am in Iraq or Texas. In Jeremiah 10:23 it says **"I know, O Lord, that a man's way is not in himself, nor is it for a man to direct his steps."** I truly believe that God can lead me to a mortar if that is His will or He can lead me away. He will direct my steps.

Job shows a trust I desire to have: **"Though He slay me, I will hope in Him"** (Job 13:15).

Soli Deo Gloria

More thoughts to come

JUNE 2, 2005

Rain on the Righteous

The other night I was clearing a man for air evacuation from Iraq to Germany. He had been injured in a rocket attack. He was minding his own business and was just leaving the PX (military equivalent to Walmart) in Baghdad. The rocket hit very near him and the shrapnel damaged his leg and his chest.

I was asking what had happened to him and how he as feeling. As he was finishing his story he started to cry and in an almost pleading way asked "What did I do wrong? Why did this happen to me? It didn't happen to anyone else

in my unit." Again and again, through sobs, he
asked, "What did I do wrong?" I assured him
that I did not think that he had done anything
wrong that brought about this injury. He and
I didn't discuss it, but we all know that each
and everyone of us have done many things
wrong. Just as the Bible says in Romans, "**for
all have sinned and fall short of the glory of
God" (Romans 3:23).** Of course, as he was
crying I was trying to think of what I could say
to him to encourage him about this apparent
injustice that had befallen him. I knew that
this was not the time to get into a many hour
discussion about how we are punished, who
gets punished, and when we will be punished
for our less than admirable deeds. Obviously,
many people feel that anything that happens
to them that is bad is a result of "bad things"
they have done. I am pretty sure that this man
was genuinely confused. I would imagine that
he thought that, although he wasn't perfect,
that, all in all, he was not doing that badly. He
was serving his country in the military and not
complaining about being in Iraq.

What could I encourage him with? The verse
that came to mind was Jesus speaking about
His father in Matthew 5:**45: "for He causes
His sun to rise on the evil and the good,
and sends the rain on the righteous and the
unrighteousness."** The chaplain was listening
to me as I shared this and as I quoted this
verse to the soldier he joined me. I explained
that this verse from the Bible showed that bad
things happen to both the good and the bad. I
then said to the soldier that the chaplain would

be here so he could talk some more about his feeling. How I wish I didn't have so many other patients to see, so I could have spent more time with him.

What else do I wish that I could have said to him? I really wanted to get into a long discourse of how I believe often God allows suffering for our eternal benefit. The verses that come to mind are from the book of Peter. 1 Peter 4:19 says **"Therefore, those also who suffer according to the will of God shall entrust their souls to a faithful Creator in doing what is right."** 1 Peter 5:10 says **"After you have suffered for a little while, the God of all grace, who called you to His eternal glory in Christ, will Himself perfect, confirm, strengthen, and establish you."**

Once again I think it comes down to trusting in a faithful Creator doing what is best for our eternal interests and not just our temporal interests.

To me the question for all of us is this: Do we trust God when the rockets of life blow up and injure us?

Soli Deo Gloria

More thoughts to come

JUNE 3, 2005

Self Destruction

A recent headline in the *Star and Stripes* stated that 27 Iraqis had died and 118 had been wounded. The majority of people involved were Iraqi police officers that were protesting the decision that a special unit was being disbanded. The protest was peaceful. The protest in Iraq is something that was rarely seen in Iraq during the Saddam years due to his heavy and lethal hand in dealing with protestors. The stadium that is in the middle of our base in Balad is very nice and was previously used for soccer games. The groundskeeper for the stadium remained even after Saddam was overthrown. Today he tells a very tragic story of the past. During the halftime of soccer games, Saddam would have people who had voiced opposition to his leadership brought to center field. He would then have their heads chopped off in front of the entire crowd.

Back to the Iraqi police who were attacked. There were two suicide bombers. The first one exploded and then as people who were not killed or severely injured were fleeing to safety the second suicide bomber joined the new crowd and then detonated himself about a minute later.

The people responsible called themselves Al Qaida, Iraq. They stated that the police were secretly promoting a pro-Israel agenda. This was of course complete nonsense, but if you are going to kill your own people then you need a justification and the one used for this attack was calling the police Jewish collaborators.

What can be said of this type of self-destruction? What would motivate people to not only kill others but also themselves? I believe the answer is told in the book of John. Jesus is telling his disciples what is coming in the future and what they can expect: **"but an hour is coming for everyone who kills you to think he is offering service to God"** (John 16:12).

It appears what is happening here as well as in Israel is the fulfillment of this prophecy of Christ.

I believe what we are engaged in here is part of a war that is being fought on many different realms. I believe at the most basic level this is a war over the spiritual direction of the world. I believe that Ephesians 6:12 speaks much of the battle that we do not see: **"For our struggle is not against flesh and blood, but against the rulers, against the powers, against the world forces of this darkness, against the spiritual forces of wickedness in the heavenly places."**

Even though we are engaged in a battle in Iraq, Israel and Jerusalem are still inextricably linked to the conflict. As it says in Psalm 122:6, "Pray for the peace of Jerusalem."

Soli Deo Gloria

More thoughts to come

JUNE 6, 2005

We Were Soldiers

I just finished watching "We Were Soldiers," a war movie based on the true story of Lt. Col. Hal Moore. The movie is an incredible war movie. I would consider it one of the best. But what stood out for me, what made this movie different than any other war movie, was how it captured the women that were left behind. It captured the pain of being left behind with no knowledge when and if they would see their husbands again.

This movie touched me in a new way this time as I watched it, mostly because now I have seen men that will not make it home or men that will make it home badly damaged. As I watched this movie I thought more of the wives and the families left behind during this conflict. I think of the newlywed wife who hears that her new husband will not return and that she is a widow even before her first anniversary. I think of the children who will not have a father. I think of the parents that will not have a son to help them as they age.

I also think about all those who will come back less than when they left. What about the father who was the proud coach of his son's soccer team who now has no legs? What about the uncle who was teaching his nephew how to throw a curve ball who now cannot use his hands because of the burns he received when an IED blew up his Humvee?

Please let us pray for all of those that are grieving. Let us pray for the wives, the sons, the daughters, the parents and all of the families that have suffered loss. Every time a suicide bomber takes out a convoy or soldiers training Iraqi soldiers, that is one less suicide bomber that can harm the homeland. These soldiers over here are sacrificing themselves for their homeland. Some are sacrificing themselves literally and all have sacrificed themselves figuratively serving in a foreign land in harm's way.

I would encourage everyone to watch this movie, even if it hurts, especially if it hurts. If you think it is too gruesome, still watch it. It is at least that gruesome here. There is an incredible scene in the deleted scenes section of the DVD. It is called "The Church". During this scene one of the wives is singing the offertory at church while her husband is in Viet Nam. The song she is singing is the hymn that has as its chorus "On Christ the Solid Rock I stand, All other ground is sinking sand, All other ground is sinking sand."

The woman is unable to get through the song and then all of the other wives join in to help. It is very powerful and there is no greater hymn to state the ultimate truth.

Soli Deo Gloria

More thoughts to come

JUNE 7, 2005

From the mouths of babes

As I was walking by an injured soldier lying
on a litter, there was a small piece of paper
with a flag drawn with crayon. It was a letter
sent from one of thousands of children who
have sent letters. I wanted to share a few of
these letters with you. There are magnificent
masterpieces or just simple words of love. I
have chosen the simple to share. Most have
backwards letters, with a mixture of upper
and lower case letters, obviously written by
children.

Dear Soldier, Thank you for protecting us. I
hope you get better. Jesus loves you. Come
home soon. Love Tawny

Dear Soldier, I hope you feel better. I really
love you because you are protecting us people
from the Iraq place. Love Ryan

Dear Soldier, I hope you feel better. Thank you
for protecting our world. Love Nicole

Dear Soldier, Thank you for keeping us safe.
Thank you saving our country. I love you.
Love Cameron

Dear Army Guy, I am sorry that you got hurt. I
love you for protecting. Tank you very much.
Love John

From Adam Lee to a Soldier: God Loves You

Soldiers, You are brave. I hope you feel well.
I think about you. I love you. Forgive the bad
people. From Connor

Soldiers, I am sorry for them when they got
bombs and when they got shot and when they
got hurt. I am sorry. Andrew K

Get well soon soldiers. I hope you feel better
soon. My daddy works in the Air Force. He
does good work. Andrew B

This last one captures how I feel when I see the
wounded:

Dear Soldier, I hope you feel Jesus loves you!
I am sorry your hurt. Thank you. Be safe.
Thank you for taking care of our country. Love
McKenzie

Soli Deo Gloria

More thought to come

JUNE 9, 2005

The Pilot

The other day after Operation Matador, there
was an increase in the number of injured
soldiers and Marines. They usually are
transitioned at least a few hours in our facility
before they are transferred to a plane for
evacuation to Germany. During this time, it
is possible to talk with the injured warriors
and get their firsthand perspective as I am

clearing them to fly and making sure their pain is under control. During this particular day, I had heard many of the stories of the hand-to-hand and house-to-house fighting that was going on. Many of the injured servicemen had been ambushed. For every unit that is on the ground going to door to door, there are also helicopters and jets supporting the troops from the air. They are there to watch and protect and intervene as indicated.

As day became evening an F-16 fighter pilot and one of the flight surgeons assigned to his unit came by to talk to the troops. He was one of the pilots that was flying high above the action and supporting the troops on the ground during the recent offensive. It was very touching to watch this pilot walk from litter to litter talking with each of the injured. I watched from a distance as he asked what had happened to each of the wounded. He then explained that he was watching out for them from high above. As I watched his face, it was not the usual sympathetic face of one of the medics. His face showed signs of taking each wounded soldier as someone he was responsible for. I could imagine that, as his task was to support these troops from the air, he felt that each soldier that he saw that had been injured was in some way his failure.

When I talked to the flight surgeon, she commented that the pilot had been very quiet after talking to the troops. She thought that the experience had affected him deeply. I was very impressed that this pilot was willing to come and talk with these brave men. It is sometimes said of pilots that since they are so far removed from the action of the infantry that they are involved in a sanitized type of warfare. I personally think this is nonsense. However, this was the first pilot I had seen come face to face with the wounded that just hours before he had been protecting. There was definitely something different about this man.

A couple weeks later I was leaving church and a man in a flight suit called to me. It was that same pilot and he thanked me again for allowing him to visit the troops. Somehow it didn't surprise me to see him at church.

Two nights ago around 11pm I was sitting at my desk in the tent where we hold the patients waiting to be aerovac'd out. The pilot came up and asked if he could go and talk with the injured again. How impressive. This wasn't a guy doing a once a year journey to the soup kitchen to absolve his guilt. There weren't any press or photographers around. He had come after work when most were sleeping. He really cared about these men and felt responsibility for them. I believe this made him a better pilot. I think he is a great example of true compassion. He probably is learning that from His Savior.

Soli Deo Gloria

More thoughts to come

JUNE 13, 2005

Not without my men

I was seeing a soldier in the hospital who was being aerovac'd out to Germany. He had been in a gun battle and had received a gunshot wound to his left arm. The bullet entered near his elbow and had torn off a whole bunch of muscle and skin before exiting down by his wrist.

I was making sure that he was ready to fly and that his pain was in good control. I was also encouraging him that in just a few hours he would be breathing the wonderfully cool, crisp air of Germany and enjoying the wonderful trees. Being in the desert makes you appreciate cool air and trees. But he looked at me with sadness in his face and said, "Yeah, that sounds nice, but my men will still be here." What an unselfish attitude. Here was a man whose arm was torn apart from a bullet and had lots of reason to feel sorry for himself and to feel entitled to some better living conditions, but his thoughts were for the men that would be left behind. I was humbled.

When I loaded him on the plane and told him to have a nice trip, tears filled his eyes. I am not sure what made him tear up, but I was wondering if his thoughts had returned to his men.

This episode brought back the thoughts of the movie "We Were Soldiers." Lt. Col. Hal Moore, at the end of the movie, has tears in his eyes as he prepares to leave the battlefield, after many of his men had died. He says "I will never forgive myself that my men died and I didn't." Both of these men were examples of selflessness and honor.

I daily witness men who teach me what it means to have honor and to be selfless. In these moments of instruction I realize how much I care for myself more than others. The thought brings me back to Christ. **"But God demonstrates His own love toward us, in that, while we were yet sinners, Christ died for us" (Romans 5:8)"**

Soli Deo Gloria

More thoughts to come

JUNE 15, 2005

Babylon

My flying today took my over the areas of Southern Iraq. I flew over ancient Babylon and the ancient home of Abraham. It is unbelievable to actually fly over these cities that I have read so much about in the Old Testament. I have heard from others that trips to the Holy Lands make the Bible come alive. I really understand now.

As I think of Babylon, the great empire that took the Jews into captivity, four people come to mind that had a similar experience here: Daniel, Shadrach, Meschach, and Abednego. Daniel 1:17 says, **"As for these four youths,**

God gave knowledge and intelligence in every branch of literature and wisdom; Daniel even understood all kinds of visions and dreams."

Shadrach, Meschach, and Abednego were made administrators over the province of Babylon. And when an order came down to from King Nebuchadnezzar that people should only worship the gold image he had made, they did not follow it rather they decided to stay faithful to the one true God. When Nebuchadnezzar heard that they did not worship the idol he was enraged and ordered them to be thrown into a fiery furnace. They responded to the decree: **"If it be so, our God whom we serve is able to deliver us from the furnace of blazing fire; and He will deliver us out of your hand, O king. But even if he does not, let it be known to you, O king, that we are not going to serve your gods or worship the golden image that you have set up"** (Daniel 3:17-18).

They were all thrown into the furnace that was heated so hot that the men throwing them in were burned to death. When the King looked into the furnace, he said, **"He said, 'Look! I see four men loosed walking about in the midst of the fire, and the appearance of the fourth looks like the son of the gods!"** (Daniel 3:25).

After the three men were removed from the fire, Nebuchadnezzar worshipped their God. **"Now I, Nebuchadnezzar, praise and exalt and honor the King of heaven, for all of His works are true and His ways are just, and He is able** to humble those who walk in pride." (Daniel 4:37).

Years later Daniel was in a similar situation, when men who were jealous of Daniel had King Darius sign a decree ordering that no one was to pray to anyone besides the king. Daniel was eventually thrown in a lion's den because he prayed to God, as was his custom, three times a day and he did not pray to the king. When Daniel survived the night in the lion's den, King Darius was also moved to worship the God of Daniel. Daniel 6:26 **"I make a decree that in all the dominion of my kingdom men are to fear and tremble before the God of Daniel"** (Daniel 6:26a).

My thoughts about these men are mostly of admiration. I also think they have an eternal exhortation for us. They easily could have gone along with the crowd. They were men in exile. As the saying goes, "when in Rome, do as the Romans do". However, they would not worship any god, but only the one true God, even to the point of death. As I sit in this land that is filled with many who hate all that is Christian or Jewish, I pray that God will raise up modern day Daniels, Shadrachs, Meshachs, and Abedengos that will testify and remain faithful to God even to the point of death and that God may use them to change the minds of even kings.

Soli Deo Gloria

More thoughts to come

JUNE 14, 2005

Jonah

I was able to go and fly around Northern Iraq the other day. I had been interested in traveling up north for one specific reason. I wanted to go to Mosul. For those who do not know, Mosul is the ancient city of Nineveh. The area is lush with vegetation as the Tigris River runs through the city. This is the city that God called Jonah to go and prophecy to. Jonah did not want to go and instead took to the ocean and was eventually swallowed by a whale. I spoke of this event in a previous "Thoughts from the Cradle".

My thoughts now go to why Jonah did not want to go to Nineveh and what his attitude was toward the **people when he finally did go.**

God says to Jonah in Jonah 1:2 "Arise, go to Nineveh the great city and cry against it, for their wickedness has come up before me." We learn later that Jonah did not go because he did not want God to forgive the Ninevites. When Jonah eventually made it to Nineveh, he proclaimed that God would overturn the city. This caused the city to repent and turn from their evil ways. Jonah 3:10 says, **"When God saw what their deeds, that they turned from their wicked way, then God relented concerning the calamity which He had declared He would bring upon them. And He did not do it."** But Jonah 4:1 says **"But it greatly displeased Jonah and he became angry."** Jonah

was angry because God showed compassion
on Nineveh after they had repented. Jonah
did not want them to be forgiven. In the last
verse of the book (Jonah 4:11), God explains
why he was compassionate: **"Should I not
have compassion on Nineveh, the great city in
which there are more than 120,000 people who
do not know the difference between their right
hand and left hand, as well as many animals?"**
God of course is talking about those who for
whatever reason are unable to understand very
simple concepts such as even right from left:
the young, the unintelligent and even animals.

I think about all of the people in the US that
think what we are doing here is not just. It
seems that they like Jonah do not want the
Iraqis to have the benefits of a society like
ours, much like Jonah not wanting the ancient
"Iraqis" to benefit from God's forgiveness and
compassion.

What I think about everyday are all the people
who are not living in fear of Saddam's death
squads, the children who get to go to school
and get immunized, the women who have
freedom to vote and further their education,
and the Olympians who can perform and not
fear having body parts cut off if they do not
win...all because the U.S. and a few of its
allies were willing to stand up and stop the
killing and the terror that reigned during the
Saddam regime.

We expect a certain level of civility in our
country. Are we unwilling to help others in

achieving the same level of civility in their country?

I am proud to say that I am involved in this effort and I look forward to the day when the Iraqi people will feel free to worship the one true God and to ask for forgiveness, just as we are able and just as the people of Nineveh did thousands of years ago.

Soli Deo Gloria

More thoughts to come

JUNE 19, 2005

Father's Day

I was flying with the Blackhawk aerovac unit the other night. We went to Baghdad to pick up a couple of soldiers who had been injured. As we were about to pick up the two men, the pilot was informed that there was a civilian contractor at a neighboring base who needed a ride to Balad to visit his son who had been injured in an IED blast. After picking up the patients from Baghdad we left for the next base. We landed and the flight medic went to get the father. He was nowhere to be found. We waited 10 minutes and then checked again but still no father. We needed to get the two wounded members back to Balad so we left. We were flying at night. We all had night vision goggles on. The whole world becomes green with halos around any light source. It is quite amazing to be able to see in the dark.

We arrived at the hospital drop off and the two patients would be on their way to Germany in just hours. I had encouraged the soldiers before we left Baghdad that they would soon be breathing fresh cool air and would have plenty of trees to see and enjoy. They smiled. It is amazing what a desert does to make you appreciate simple pleasures. I completely forgot about the father who is trying to get to his son's side.

The following day I was in the patient ward of the hospital. I was clearing patients for flights to Kuwait and Germany with one of the other flight surgeons. I started talking to one of the patients who seemed to have a good sense of humor. He had sustained a knee injury when his Bradley vehicle rolled across a very big bomb. He described that blast like God had picked up his Bradley, a multi-ton heavily armored vehicle, shook it and then threw it down. His Bradley had been involved in more than 20 IED blasts. This one would be its last. His knee was injured and he had many other cuts and bruises on his body. He said that his commander said, "I am glad that you are OK. I am also thankful that you guys in the Bradley hit the bomb and not a Humvee because they would have all been killed." The soldier agreed with the commander. The armor of the Bradley had saved the lives of himself and his crew and probably some unknowing Humvee crew.

I asked him how he was feeling and if his pain was under control. He said the pain was not too bad. He had been able to talk to his wife before the official military phone call had notified her that her husband had been injured in combat. He then went on to volunteer that what really helped him was seeing his father. He explained that his father was a civilian contractor in Iraq and that the military had flown him in last night to see him. It meant the world to him because he had not seen his father in two years. Previous to this deployment he had been in Korea for 18 months. It was nice to be able to tell him that the Army was trying so hard to get his father to Balad that they had diverted our helo to go and try to pick him up also. I know it was an incredible blessing to this soldier to have his father visit. I was blessed to be able to see both sides of the story.

I do not know what kind of relationship this son and father had, but I am pretty sure when your child has been injured all that matters is the present. The past becomes largely irrelevant. It reminds of the relationship between Absalom and David. Even though Absalom tried to take the kingdom away from his Father, David mourned greatly when his son was killed in battle against the king's soldiers: " **O my son Absalom! My son, my son Absalom! Would I had died instead of you, O Absalom, my son, my son**" (2 Samuel 18:33).

A special thanks to all the Fathers who are serving today and heartfelt condolences for all those Fathers who have outlived their children.

Soli Deo Gloria

More thoughts to come

JUNE 25, 2005

Sufficient Grace

I will be completely honest with you. Working
with the wounded day after day is starting
to affect me. I first noticed it when I went to
clear a patient for flight who had been in a
tank accident. He had just come back from
surgery. A tank tread had hit him in the chest,
shoulder and head. His scapula, the shoulder
blade bone, was broken in half. This is very
rare and indicates severe trauma. His had
what is called a right "flail chest", which
means that as he tried to inhale that part would
not move because of multiple broken ribs.
Those were his minor injuries compared to
his back and head. His first lumber vertebra
was split in half and he would most likely be
a paraplegic. He had at least two fractures of
his cervical vertebrae. But, worst of all, the
neurosurgeon was forced to take off half of
his skull and the entire left side of his brain
would probably not function again. I had seen
really bad trauma before, so what made this
one different? First, he looked like a grown-up
version of my almost 17-year-old son. Second,
his commander asked me what he should tell
his wife. With those issues, I was fully hit with
the weight of the news that this unsuspecting
wife was about to receive. There was not an
easy way to sugarcoat his injuries and the team
wasn't even sure whether he could survive the
head injury. The commander wanted to know
if he should get the wife to Germany or if he
was only going to stay a few hours in Germany

before being flown to the US and should she
wait for her husband there. He also asked to
be kept in the loop in case the soldier needed
to be medically retired if his death looked
imminent. The military will often medically
retire a soldier who is about to die from a
medical condition so that his family is entitled
to benefits for the rest of their life. During this
time, as I looked on the broken masterpiece
of God, I was to the point of tears. I am never
sure when a patient will really affect me or
why they do, but this soldier did. And they are
affecting me more and more. I will give you a
brief partial look through my eyes over the last
48 hours so you can visualize and pray for the
hurting over here:

Man with both arms blown off and lungs badly
damaged by the blast

Five women all with severe burns when their
truck was hit by a suicide bomber carrying
a propane tank—four of the five were on
ventilators due to inhaling hot gas into their
lungs

Man on a ventilator that had been hit with
a bullet that had entered his hip and exited
through his opposite chest

Man who how has a tracheostomy and is on a
ventilator because he was hit by an IED and
the shrapnel hit his neck, damaging vessels and
other structures

Woman barely surviving on a ventilator who
was hit by an IED—her spleen was badly

damaged and needed to be removed, her right diaphragm was destroyed, she had multiple injuries to her intestines, and her lungs were badly damaged

Man whose face was crushed when someone threw a large truck through the windshield of the truck he was driving

So what will I do now that, after two months, I feel that caring for all of the injured is starting to affect me? I have two choices: I can become callous and choose not to feel or I can encourage myself in God's word:

"And He said to me, 'My grace is sufficient for you, for power is perfected in weakness. Most gladly, therefore, I will boast about my weaknesses so that the power of Christ may dwell in me'" (2 Corinthians 12:9).

"Let us not lose heart in doing good, for in due time we will reap if we do not grow weary" (Galatians 6:9).

I will choose to be encouraged by God's word and let tears come as they may.

Soli Deo Gloria

More thoughts to come

JUNE 27, 2005

Close Ranks

In my last TFTC, I wrote about the some of the injured I have seen in the last few days. I am not sure if everyone is aware of the term "close ranks". It is used in military operations when there is a battle line. When some of the soldiers in the line are injured, then the soldiers are to "close ranks", which means to join once again shoulder to shoulder to fill in the gaps left by the wounded or killed. You can see it best demonstrated in movies like "The Patriot" when they fight side by side. We do not fight like that anymore but the term still applies in a figurative sense in that when it gets tough, you get closer as a unit. If a group of men are surrounded, they will huddle together to help save each other. Now the military is made up of ordinary people. There are some people in your unit that you like and some that you really wish were in a different unit. But when the fighting starts and your unit is in harm's way, then all of the disagreements over religion, politics, sports teams, and which NASCAR car is better (Ford or Chevy) start to fall away and you try to survive and encourage each other to have the courage to fight, even to the death.

So why am I saying all of this? Well, I am not sure that everyone in the States is aware that we get quite a bit of news over here. We don't get as much as in the States and those who are in forward locations may get even less, but at most bases there is a daily *Stars and Stripes* newspaper and CNN and/or Fox news is on Air Force Network TV. We see American blood on the floor of the operating room or the ICU or in the back of a helicopter and we see men crying because they have lost a buddy. In that same day or hour, when we have a chance to

read a *Stars or Stripes* or watch some TV over
a meal, we get to hear how less than 50% of
the public support what we are doing. Let there
be no mistake. The phrase "I support the troops
but do not support the war" are empty words.
When I hear someone say that expression,
which is frequently, I in no way feel supported.
In fact, I take it as a statement that they are
against what I am doing. So how can they
support me without supporting what I am
doing? I believe support for me and my role
here are inextricably linked.

It is a tough battle over here trying to fight
an enemy who will kill themselves to kill
us, an enemy who doesn't care if innocent
civilians get killed. However, if we happen to
accidentally kill an innocent person, then the
media wants immediate punishment of the
soldier. With the fall of support for the war
for freedom for Iraq, I sense the battle lines in
America are starting to break.

Now is not the time to debate this war, which
I believe is just. That can be done later. While
there are men and women in harm's way, I
ask one thing of all those who are enjoying
the freedom of the U.S. who will enjoy the
fireworks of Independence Day, who go to the
store without the fear of a car bomb, who will
enjoy a picnic and a BBQ this 4th of July:

CLOSE RANKS.

Soli Deo Gloria

More thoughts to come

JUNE 29, 2005

Three Conversations

The other day I had the privilege of having three great conversations on the same day. The first was with a Marine Corporal who had been on the front lines going house to house looking for bad guys and weapons, the next was with an Iraqi Colonel and, to finish the night, the last was with a female Marine who was in the back of a truck that was hit by a suicide bomber.

The Marine

I was doing my usual hospital duties of clearing patients to be aerovac'd out. As I was finishing, I overheard a Marine asking where a certain location was. He then asked how long of a walk it was. I joined the conversation and said it was about 1-2 miles. He started to leave on crutches, determined to find a buddy of his who was here and who he hadn't had the chance to say goodbye to nearly a year ago. I have absolute respect for the toughness of Marines, but I could not bear to let him walk two miles on crutches. I asked him if he wanted a ride and he accepted, with a certain disbelief that a Lt. Col. would give him a ride.

As we rode I asked where he was stationed and what type of activity he was involved in. He went on to explain to me that he was in the infantry and he was going house to house searching for bad guys and weapons. His unit was in the west near the Syrian border. He explained what it was like going door to door. He said his battalion had suffered 28 KIAs (killed in action). He described his Major standing behind a concrete wall and when a rocket hit the wall a chunk of concrete hit the Major's chest with such force that it was essentially removed from the rest of his body. The Corporal had become very disenchanted with how much the civilians lied about their innocence and now he considered every Arab a bad guy until proven otherwise. He told me of an incident where two of the Sergeants in his unit were in a house they thought was clear. The occupants had proclaimed they were innocent. Then anti-aircraft guns that were hidden underneath the floor started firing, instantly killing the two Sergeants. He explained to me that he was injured jumping over a barricade when he came under mortar attack and then hurt his hand jumping back to the other side when more firing started. He said that he had no idea how anyone would act when fired upon. He stated that his fellow Marines have said that in the middle of fire fights that he has killed enemies; however, he has no recollection of killing anyone. He said that almost everyone they were confronting in the west were not Iraqis but Syrians and other foreigners who have lots of cash to recruit bombers for missions.

We eventually got to the squadron where his buddy was supposed to be, not at all where he had thought it was. It was good that he didn't walk or crutch there. His buddy was no longer there. Charlie Company had moved to the

north. The Marine was clearly disappointed
not to be able to see his buddy. I sensed he
felt very alone and very numb from all he
had been through. He talked with almost
no emotion, just matter of factly. I was also
disappointed that we did not find his buddy
but I was blessed to have had the chance to
talk to this very brave young man. I have been
very impressed with the young men fighting
this war and I consider it a great honor to serve
with them. I hope when people see a member
of the Armed Forces they take the time to ask
them what their thoughts are. There is much to
be appreciated about these brave warriors and
their perspective is firsthand, as opposed to the
thoughts of people who have never ventured
out of the think tanks of Washington DC.

The Iraqi Colonel

That night at dinner an Iraqi Colonel and his
translator sat at our table. We were having
our conversation and they were having theirs.
I really wanted to talk to the Colonel and,
after everyone had finished eating, I asked the
interpreter where he was from. He was from
Dearborn, Michigan and of Lebanese descent.
I asked the Colonel the same question and
he said "Babylon". Imagine having Babylon
as your hometown. I asked him how the
rebuilding of Babylon was coming along. This
question started him down a long explanation
of the recent history of Iraq. He explained how
Babylon was being rebuilt just about the same
time the Iran/Iraq war started. He explained
that it was a very difficult war and that neither

side won. The war ended as a tired draw. He went on to add that all of the money in the country over the last 20 years has been spent on war materials and that the infrastructure of the country has gone lacking. He then stated, "Well, you know that after the Iran war, we were in two wars with the U.S. You watched the news. You know we ran when we faced you in battle. But now we are Brothers." He said that last sentence with a big smile on his face. What a professional soldier. Professional soldiers do not hold grudges against their enemy. They realize that war is between the nations not between the individuals; therefore, when the fighting is over it is possible to be "brothers".

Our conversation then transitioned into the future of Iraq. The gist of his comments were twofold: 1) he thought there will be much less insurgency once Saddam is executed and 2) he knows most of the insurgency is from outside Iraq, sponsored with money that Saddam had hidden during his reign. He also added that Saddam signaled the insurgency to start when, three months after the collapse of Baghdad, he said, "The battle will now begin".

It was great to talk with an Iraqi who was so well versed in the history of not only the country but the military as well. One of the last statements he made before we said goodbye was, "All we need is one year of peace and you will be amazed what Iraqis can do to improve their country." I pray that peace will come.

The Female Marine

After dinner I went back to the contingency
areomedical staging facility or CASF. This is
where those who are injured are prepared for
the plane flight out. Think of it as an airport
terminal with wounded as the passengers and
nurses, techs and docs as the service providers.
Oh yeah, there are no Starbucks or Sbarro's
anywhere in sight.

One of the patients I needed to clear for flight
was a female Marine. She must have been
around 20 years old, 5"6" and about 110
pounds soaking wet. She had a neck brace on
and, as I approached her, she was commenting
on how tough she was even though she was
relatively small. I saw from her paperwork
that she was in injured after the truck she was
riding in was targeted by a suicide bomber. She
had a stable fracture of her neck and a couple
of burns on her fingers but was otherwise in
good shape. I asked her how her pain was and
she repeated, "I am tough. I don't need any
pain medication." She smiled as she said she
was tough and you could tell she had a great
sense of humor, but there was no mistaking
that she was a Marine.

She then explained to me what happened to
the truck that she was riding on. The truck was
carrying female Marines who were involved
in searching female Iraqis going through
checkpoints. This is another example of how
we have been bending over backwards to
maintain sensitivity to the culture here. Their

shift was over and they were on their way back
to their base. A car drove up along the truck and
a man got out. He had a number of incendiary
devices and was carrying a propane tank like
we would use with a gas grill. In an instant,
he blew himself up. The truck was instantly
involved in a fireball that followed the blast.
The Marine remembers feeling very hot and
then waking up outside the truck. She looked
around at those with her. There were at least
three dead and she could see the skin dripping
off the bodies of many of the others. The
woman to the right of her was severely burned.
I had actually sent that woman to Germany a
couple nights before on a ventilator and with
severe burns to her hands and face. The woman
to the left of her had bad burns to her face but
was not on a ventilator and was also on her way
to the burn center in San Antonio via Germany.
The Marine maintained a great attitude during
the entire conversation and couldn't believe
how little she was hurt. As she was explaining
how little she was injured compared to those
around her she stated, "Jesus must have been
giving me a big hug." Most people would
consider a broken neck a pretty big injury, but
compared to her friends she had it good. She
said that she was doing well but thought that
she would never forget the sight of dripping
skin. She wondered why more hadn't happened
to her when so many of her friends had been
so severely injured. She also wondered if this
would screw her up in the future. What do you
say to a person who has witnessed what she
had and then questions why she survived and

her friends didn't? I am not sure what the best thing is to say. I took the cue from her saying that "Jesus was hugging her" and I encouraged her that it did appear that God had protected her for some reason. I told her I did not know what that reason was, but that I believed that we all have a God-prescribed purpose and it is our job to seek God and find out what that purpose is. Some never find their purpose and some find it and choose not to fulfill it. Then there are those who seek God and follow wherever He leads. Those are the people that I find to be the most content with their lives.

So I spoke with three very different people with three very different perspectives. I really enjoyed this day and I felt privileged to have spoken with such quality people in a single day.

As I close this long discourse on my experiences that day, I want to add how I was encouraged by the recent speech by President Bush and I am sure the Iraqi Colonel would be as well. The President was discussing that many had called on us to pull out of Iraq before it was stable. His answer was firm: "For the sake of our nation's security, this will not happen on my watch." No opinion polls support this decision. This is a decision of a brave and great leader, who cares more about the future of America than his poll numbers. I am honored to serve under his command.

Soli Deo Gloria

More thoughts to come

JULY 1, 2005

Why Desert?

I have flown over much of the country of Iraq. I am impressed at how beautiful parts of the country are and also how stark and desolate it can be just a few miles away. I have already written before about the life-giving water and how where there is water it is green and beautiful and where the water stops so does the lushness.

The contrast in environments got me wondering if it always looked this way when Adam, Eve, Abraham, Noah and Jonah walked this land. If it has always looked this way, that led me to think of what was God trying to teach the early men and women by putting them specifically in this environment. He could have chosen the Amazon rainforest or Yosemite Valley or some Hawaiian island. But He did not. He chose a place with quite a bit of desert. The desert is an awesome place. Its heat during the summer is overpowering. It has already been up to 122 here and the high is expected to reach in the 130's. The local culture does little outside during the heat of the summer day and from what I have read this has been true for thousands of years. So what is God's purpose for putting the first men and women in this kind of climate? They could have been in a place where they could climb trees and explore the forest or hike through the mountains and pastures or swim in beautiful Pacific waters. I know God always has a purpose and my mind wondered what that might be for this to be chosen as the "cradle of civilization". God seems to like to have people wander through the desert when He is trying to teach them or mature them. Only once they have matured are they allowed to enter the "promised land".

I thought of what God desires of us. In Micah 6:8 that question is answered, **"He has told you, O man, what is good; and what does the Lord require of you but to do justice, to love kindness and to walk humbly with your God?"** I can act justly and love mercy anywhere I am, but what does it take to walk humbly with God? A few things come to mind: 1) time that is free from distractions (I find distractions often have a way of getting my eyes off God and on whatever I have involved myself with), 2) quietness to hear God, 3) a respect for the smallness of us compared to God, and 4) the ability and necessity to wait on God. As I look at this list the desert is a great place for each of these. The barrenness of the desert is relatively free from distraction. There are no beautiful tropical fish to stare at for hours. There are few sounds in the desert, besides wind, to cloud our minds. I do not hear birds or insects or other animals, but just wind. The vastness of the desert lets one realize just how small we are, especially if you think of God using the Earth as his footstool. Finally, the heat of the desert gives one much time to wait on God to speak. It is so hot during the midday sun that one is forced to be still and wait for cooler temperature.

Once again I am convinced that God is much more concerned with our eternal home and happiness than the comforts of everyday life. This is especially true when those very comforts can distract us from walking humbly with Him.

I find it very hard to be still and wait and listen for God. I have quite a bit of free time in the evenings. God has given me a **choice: "Cease striving and know that I am God" (Psalm 46:10) or find a thousand** and one things that I can be active with, such as watching DVDs exercising, playing games and so on. He also exhorts me to wait on Him: **"Wait for the Lord; be strong and let your heart take courage; yes, wait for the Lord"** (Psalm 27:14). However, I often find myself wanting to get things done in my timing instead of His.

My soul longs for the quietness and the peace of the desert to walk humbly with God, but my flesh with its pride wants nothing of idleness. The man in me would rather be busy with pleasures and activities that make me feel important. I have found in my own life that if I do not make arrangement for time in the figurative desert, God will do it for me…and sometimes it ends up being the real desert.

Soli Deo Gloria

More thoughts to come

JULY 3, 2005

Staying with the supplies

As we have approached the fourth of July
there have many that take this time to thank
those serving in the military for what they are
doing to maintain America's freedoms. These
voices of appreciation are great to hear and
for the most part I feel I am being thanked for
just doing my job. I do not feel that I am doing
anything that is especially brave or heroic, but
just my assignment. All the same, it is great to
get such wonderful support from friends and
families and people who value the military.

What I would like to do is share a story from
the Bible because I feel it has special relevance
to today.

"When David came to the two hundred men
who were too exhausted to follow David, who
had been left at the brook Besor, and they
went out to meet David and to meet the people
who were with him, then David approached
the people and greeted them. Then all of the
wicked and worthless men among those who
went with David said, 'because they did not go
with us, we will not give them any of the spoil
that we have recovered,except to every man
his wife and his children, that they may lead
them away and depart. Then David replied,
'You must not do so, my brothers, with what
the Lord has given us, who has kept us and
delivered into our hand the band that came
against us. And who will listen to you in this

matter? For as his share is who goes down to battle, so shall his share be who stays with the baggage; they shall share alike.'" (I Samuel 30:21-24)

I thought of this story because I think of all of those who would like to serve for the cause of freedom but cannot. I think of all of those who have already served and would like to serve again. I received an e-mail just the other day from a woman in Texas whose husband has already retired as a Lt. Col. and is trying to be reinstated so he can come and serve again. I think about those who have served valiantly in the past and all we have of them is memories.

So, with this wonderful story in my mind, I wanted to take this opportunity to thank all of those who have "stayed with the supplies". Your prayers, care packages, and letters mean the world to us over here. We may not be very good about writing back to you and thanking you for all that is being done for us back home, but know that it is appreciated.

Please continue to pray for us, especially for those troops that are going door-to-door and driving convoys.

Soli Deo Gloria

More thoughts to come

JULY 4, 2005

Independence Day

I witnessed an interesting event at the dining facility the other night and thought it was perfect to share for the Fourth of July.

The dining facility here holds probably 1000-2000 people. There are multiple cafeteria-style lines to get food from. There are tables lined up that hold about eight people each and there are TVs that are set up in the corners of the rooms usually showing news or movies on Air Force Network. The TVs are largely ignored except by those who are close to them. However, on this night it was different. After I had picked up my food I noticed that almost everyone in the facility was watching the TV. It was relatively silent so the dialogue could be heard even from far away. And many like me stopped where they were to watch what was on.

So what show had quieted the room? It was the movie "Braveheart". The specific scene that had everyone transfixed on the TV was when, at the end of the movie, William Wallace is being tortured. The entire crowd watching him being tortured is begging for him to ask for mercy. I think probably almost everyone in the room knew this movie and knew what was coming next. But we all wanted to hear it. We all wanted to see this man who was being tortured not beg for mercy but to maintain his dignity and keep faith with all those who had died before him.

So what were his last words going to be? What was he going to use his last breath to utter? What was so significant to him that he would allow it to take him to an excruciatingly painful death?

The answer came in his last word. Wallace gathered his strength and then, with a yell that echoed through the mountains, he bellowed: "FREEDOM!"

We celebrate freedom at home. We are defending it here.

Happy Fourth of July!

Soli Deo Gloria

More thoughts to come

JULY 7, 2005

Troop levels

Currently in the news there is a lot of talk about what is the right amount of troops to maintain stability in Iraq. Some will say that we have too many and others will say not enough. Still others will say we have the right number and they just need to be in different places. I do not know the answer to this question and I am pretty confident that no one knows for sure.

It is interesting that as you read the Old Testament there are a couple of interactions that God has with man regarding troop numbers that I think are very telling.

The first is God's interaction with Gideon. Gideon is about to face the Midianites and this is what God tells him: "**The Lord said to Gideon, 'The people who are with you are too many for Me to give Midian into their hands, for Israel would become boastful, saying, "My own power has delivered me.' Now therefore come, proclaim in the hearing of the people, saying, 'Whoever is afraid and trembling, let him return and depart from Mount Gilead'**" (**Judges** 7:2-3). This reduced the Israelite army from 32,000 to 10,000 men. God used two more tests to make the army smaller and eventually ended up with 300 men. This type of battle preparation makes no sense to men. However, as the word of God says, "**but God has chosen the foolish things of the world to shame the wise, and God has chosen the weak things of the world to shame the things which are strong**" (**1 Corinthians** 1:27). Of course this strategy that God used with Gideon is pure foolishness in the eyes of wise war planners.

The next interaction is between David and God. For some unknown reason David wants to count how many fighting men he has in his country. Joab tells him it is bad idea but the King insists and the men of fighting age are counted. The counting of the men brings great displeasure from God and David has to choose one of three curses as a punishment for his sin. This story is found in 2 Samuel 24 and 1 Chronicles 21. It does not say specifically why God did not want David to count his men, but I can think of two reasons: 1) knowing the number of men would cause David to put his trust in the numbers rather than in God and 2) David was likely already filled with pride over his kingdom and what he thought he had accomplished, even though it was God who had delivered the nation of Israel from the hands of enemies and blessed its growth.

Interesting that in neither story is God interested in Israel's troop strength. Additionally, in all the modern wars that Israel has been involved, they have been horribly outnumbered. Yet against all odds they have overcome and won every battle since the rebirth of their nation.

The moral to these stories is if God is on your side, leave your war calculators at home. The King of Kings and the Lord of Lords will be sufficient for whatever battle you find yourself in. This truth applies both to war and plain old life.

Soli Deo Gloria

More thoughts to come

JULY 9, 2005

Modern Day Uriah

I just finished talking with an injured soldier and his story reminded me of one of the most honorable soldiers of the Bible.

This army soldier broke his neck after a fall. His neck is unstable and he needs a special device called a halo to keep his neck from moving while the fracture heals. If he were allowed to move his neck freely he is at risk of damaging his spinal cord and possibly being paralyzed. Shortly after coming to our area he asked to see me. I approached this soldier who was laying flat on his back with a neck brace on that was secured to the bed. He could only look at the ceiling. He wanted to talk to me about his injuries. He wanted to know if he were going to have any lasting injuries. I explained that at this point it was hard to tell but the fact that he had a normal neurological exam so far was promising for his future as long as his neck was allowed to heal. His next question was shocking due to its valor. He asked, "Will I be able to come back to my unit after my neck has healed?" I responded that I wasn't sure how long it would take for him to recover and what the Army would do with him after he had recuperated. He then said, "I came here with my unit and I want to leave with my unit." What honor! Many would have used this as the ticket home. I do not think anyone would begrudge someone who has a broken neck from getting a ticket home. But this soldier was different. He had a commitment to his unit that superceded his own welfare. It would have seemed only natural for him to look forward to being done with his tour in Iraq but, no, he was committed and didn't want to break faith with his fellow soldiers.

So what famous Biblical soldier did this young man remind me of? There is one soldier who stands out in David's army who was absolutely committed to his troops above his own welfare. That man was Uriah.

In the eleventh chapter of 2 Samuel the story is told of when David's soldiers went out to war and he stayed behind. While Uriah was fighting, David slept with his wife Bathsheba and she became pregnant.

"Then David sent word to Joab saying, 'Send me Uriah the Hitite.' So Joab sent Uriah to David. When Uriah came to him, David asked concerning the welfare of Joab and the people and the state of the war. Then David said to Uriah, 'Go down to your House, and wash your feet.' And Uriah went out of the king's house, and a present from the king was sent out after him. But Uriah slept at the door of the king's house with all the servants of his lord, and did not go down to his house. Now when they told David, saying, 'Uriah did not go down to his house,' David said to Uriah, 'Have you not come from a hourney? Why did you not go down to your house?' Uriah said to David, 'The ark and Israel and Judah are staying in temporary shelters, and my lord Joab and the servants of my lord are camping in the open field. Shall I then go to my house to eat and drink and to lie with my wife? By your life and the life of your soul, I will not do this thing!' Then David said to Uriah, 'Stay here today also, and tomorrow I will you go.' So Uriah remained in Jerusalem that day and the next. Now David called him, and he ate and drank with him, and he made him drunk, and in the evening he went out to lie on his bed with his lords's servants, but he did not go down to his house." (2 Samuel 11:6-13)

Since Uriah would not sleep with his wife
and therefore David had no way to cover
the fact that David had gotten her pregnant
he eventually told Joab **"Place Uriah in the
front line of the fiercest battle and withdraw
from him so he will be struck down and die."**
(2 Samuel 11:15).

The soldier of whom I speak today is worthy
of praise, like Uriah. It humbles me to serve
with men who have such honor.

Soli Deo Gloria

More thoughts to come

JULY 12, 2005

Why are we here?

It seems like the almost constant discussion
in the news as well as over here is why are
we here? Have we won anything for the Iraqi
people or does being here just cause more
bloodshed?

I found a passage in scripture that I think
speaks to our exact situation. It comes from the
book of Nehemiah. The majority of the book
of Nehemiah is discussing the rebuilding of the
walls and the city of Jerusalem. The enemies
of Israel did not want the city rebuilt. They
first started ridiculing Israel for what they were
trying and then they started to attack Israel
while they were rebuilding. This is where we
pick up the story:

"From that day on, half of my servants carried on the work, while half of them held the spears, the shields, the bows, and the breastplates; and the captains were behind the whole house of Judah. Those who were rebuilding the wall and those who carried burdens took their load with one hand doing the work and the orther holding a weapon. As for the builders, each wore his sword girded at his side as he built, the trumpeter stood near me." (Nehemiah 4:16-18)

"So we carried on the work with half of them holding spears from dawn until the stars appeared. At that time I also said to the people, 'Let each man and his servant spend the night within Jerusalem at night so they may be a guard for us by night and a laborer by day.' So neither I, my brothers, my servants, nor the men of the guard who followed me, none of us removed our clothes, each took his weapon, even to the water." (Nehemiah 4: 21-23)

I believe just like the time of Nehemiah we are here to stand guard while the Iraqis rebuild their country. Just as in Nehemiah's time there are many enemies here who do not want Iraq to be rebuilt and do not want it to taste freedom.

So what do I think that God thinks about us being here? I would not venture to speculate on God's sovereign will; however, I am confident that our motivations are honorable and that all that is occurring will fit perfectly into His plan for the Iraqi people. It is very clear in the Old Testament that God directs both righteous

and unrighteous leaders to follow His will,
so regardless how one feels about the current
leaders, I am absolutely confident that God is
still on the throne.

Lastly, I believe that for the soldier on the
ground, what God requires of us is to do our
duty in a way that brings honor to him.

Soli Deo Gloria

More thoughts to come

JULY 14, 2005

Insurgents vs. Terrorists

In the July 13 edition of *Stars and Stripes*,
there is an article titled "ZARQAWI
QUESTIONS MENTOR'S MOTIVES:
terror mastermind warns 'our noble sheik'
against urging militants to spare civilians"
The 'noble sheik' Zarqawi was referring to
was Al-Barqawi. Al-Barqawi has recently
stated that, "the number of Iraqis killed in
suicide operations is a tragedy". To this very
reasonable and honest assessment of the
situation Zarqawi had this to say in response,
"do not follow the path of Satan that leads to
your destruction. Beware, our noble sheik, of
the trick of God's enemies to lure you to drive
a wedge in the ranks of the Mujahideen." So in
essence, Zarqawi is saying that killing innocent
civilians is following God and sparing them is
following the path of Satan. There is a verse in
the Old Testament that describes this perfectly.
The verse is found in the book of Isaiah: **"Woe**

to those who call evil good and good evil, who substitute darkness for light and light for darkness, who substitute bitter for sweet and sweet for bitter" (Isaiah 5:20).

I am very disappointed that the press has used the sanitized name "insurgents" instead of "terrorists". The followers of Zarqawi are not fighting for freedom and for the wellbeing of the people of Iraq. They are fighting for what they have lost. What have they lost? Power. Power to control the minds of the people. Power to control the resources that should make Iraq a rich nation. Money and power is what they are after. They do not care about the people and they have formed a squad of so-called martyrs to carry out their mission. If being a martyr is such a great honor why doesn't Zarqawi step forward and take his place next to all of the people who have killed themselves killing others? Now, to be fair, some of the bombers have been forced to become suicide bombers. Many of these bombers have been taken from their homes and tied to the steering wheel of a car and they are told if they do not make it to their target then their family will die as well. Regardless of who is actually doing the bombing, what type of honor is found in killing innocent people including children? There is no honor; only disgrace and cowardice. Killing children is an abomination. **"See that you do not despise one of these little ones, for I tell you that their angels in heaven continually see the face of my Father who is in heaven"** (Matthew 18:10). But Zarqawi states that this is the path that God is leading them down. We have truly entered a time when "evil is called good and good is called evil."

Just yesterday a group of soldiers were out of their Humvee giving toys and candy to children when a suicide bomber drove up and blew the car up. 27 people were killed; 12 were children. The children were in plain sight as the car approached.

What I do not understand is why the Arab world has not stood up and condemned these attacks. The killing of innocent civilians is beyond a tragedy. It is evil. If they do not want us, the U.S. Military, here in their country, that is a fair complaint. Bring the war to us. We will not run. We will stay and fight if they are insistent on fighting.

But blow up children coming for candy and toys? I cannot find words strong enough to characterize such an act. **"But Jesus said, 'Let the children alone, and do not hinder them from coming to me, for the kingdom of heaven belongs to such as these'"** (Matthew 19:14). I am confident that after the suicide bomber died he did not receive 70 virgins and feasts, as is the promise to anyone who is martyred killing infidels. **"There is a way which seems right to a man, but its end is the way of death"** (Proverbs 16:25).

Soli Deo Gloria

More thoughts to come

JULY 18, 2005

The smell of hot dogs

I went on an aerovac mission to Germany today. As flight surgeons we usually are not on aerovac missions. Our job is to make sure the patients are ready to fly with just nurses and techs. Sometimes, though, a doctor is needed for patients who require a higher level of care than the aerovac crew can offer. I was asked to be the medical attendant for a 52-year-old with a mild heart attack.

The plane was scheduled to leave around 0345, but then it was bumped to 0655. We ended up taking off around 0530. This flight was quite full. We had 18 patients on litters and 17 patients who were ambulatory.

What struck me about this mission (I have seen this before but have not written about it yet) is the care that is given to the wounded warriors by the aerovac crew. The crew flies down from Germany. The flight is around 5 hours long. On the way down, they rest. About an hour before arrival, they start to prepare the plane for patients and they continue to do this once the plane lands and the cargo are removed. The planes are not set up specifically for patients. They are made to haul cargo, human or other. If they are hauling bullets or bombs, all of these items are put on large metal pallets and then rolled into the plane. If they are hauling patients, then litter stanchions must be placed and supplied with power and oxygen. Then the patients are loaded one by one onto the plane. The litter stanchions look somewhat like bunk beds and can be as tall as five high. Tonight they were two to three high.

The patient I was monitoring was at my feet on the lowest "bunk" just six inches off the floor. Across from him was a soldier injured in an IED blast who had three metal rods on the outside of his left leg holding it together until he can be properly repaired in Germany or the U.S. The guy above him was also injured in an IED blast but his injuries were burned hands and face. This is a very common injury for the gunners in Humvees. When the blast occurs the only parts that are exposed are their face and hands and they take most of the fiery blast. There were patients to my left and to my right all with a story, all with a family anxiously waiting for their return home. The plane was loud and was either too cold or too hot. It's not a good place for Goldilocks or wounded warriors, but it's the fastest way to get these brave men and women to a medical facility that can properly care for them. There was very little complaining on the flight. Most slept.

What the aerovac crew does is to make sure every patient receives the medicine they need, as well as food, water and creative ways to go to the bathroom while laying flat on a litter. As they busily attended to each patient tonight, I started to smell cooking meat. Minutes later, hot dogs showed up. In Iraq there is no fresh bread as it is almost all sent from Kuwait or Qatar and is pretty firm by the time we get it. But the aerovac crew brought hot dogs and fresh buns from Germany. They did not have to do this. The expense is paid themselves. It is their way of caring for the troops. After the hot dogs, the smell of chocolate cookies filled the air. There is a small convection oven in the C-141, and it was used to warm the hot dogs and then bake the cookies. It may seem like a small thing but to all of us on the plane, the caring attitude was very much appreciated. On a previous flight from Germany, the loadmaster, usually not known for their gentleness, was quite the gourmet chef. He prepared a 7-course meal. It started with cheese and salami on crackers drizzled with olive oil with a peppercinni or small tomato added on top. Then there was delicious cauliflower, nicely seasoned. BBQ chicken wings, shrimp scampi and a marinated pork tenderloin finished out the meal, followed by fresh baked cookies. When asked why he did it, he simply stated that he did it for the medics. He would not accept any reimbursement for this kind act. It was his way of saying thank you. As you can imagine his care and thoughtfulness was very much appreciated and it made the flight go by quickly.

Both the aerovac crew and the loadmaster remind me of a verse: **"In everything I showed you that by working hard in this manner you must help the weak and remember the words of the Lord Jesus, that He Himself said: 'It is more blessed to give than to receive'"** (Acts 20:35).

Soli Deo Gloria

More thoughts to come

JULY 20, 2005

Patience of Job

Anytime there is suffering, such as is so
evident in times of war or terrorist attacks, one
is sure to hear the famous refrain of "Where
is God?" and "Why isn't He intervening?"
"If He is so loving and so powerful why isn't
he stopping this pain?" These are questions
I hear quite often, both as a member of the
medical contingent in Iraq, as well as when I
am back home caring for children with serious
heart defects. When I hear these statements
questioning God, I have two thoughts that go
through my mind: 1) who is man to put God on
trial? and 2) there is a thoughtful response to
these queries of God that should be stated. Just
as a husband will defend his wife or a father
defends his children, I have a strong desire to
defend God's reputation during these attacks.
My desire to defend comes from my firm belief
that God is all-knowing, all-powerful and all-
loving. I could write pages on why I know this
is true, but in the interest of being brief, I will
try to summarize as best I can.

I believe the best place to learn about God and
suffering is the book of Job. Job is a man who
God knew to be righteous. Satan came before
God and said that the only reason that Job was
righteous was because God had blessed him.
Satan contended that if Job were to suffer he
would turn from God. God allowed Satan to
cause Job to suffer by taking away his riches
and his children. Still Job did not sin. Satan

returned to God and said if You allow me to cause his body harm then Job will turn from You. God once again allowed Satan to torture Job, this time by bringing horrible diseases on his body. Still Job did not sin, but he began to question why God had allowed this tragedy to befall him. Job went on and on about how unfair this was and his three friends went on and on about how he deserved it because of his hidden sin.

Finally God speaks: "Then the Lord answered Job out of the whirlwind and said, 'Who is this that darkens counsel by words without knowledge? Now gird up your loins like a man, and I will ask you and you will instruct me. Where were you when I laid the foundation of the earth? Tell Me if you have understanding. Who set its measurements? Since you know! Or who stretched the line on it'" (Job 38:1-5)? God continues to show Job that he looks at the world from a very limited perspective where God has eternity as His perspective. Then God asks Job to answer Him. "The Lord said to Job, 'Will the faultfinder contend with the Almighty? Let him who reproves God answer it!' Then Job answered the Lord: 'I am insignificant; what can I reply to You? I lay my hand on my mouth. Once I have spoken, and I will not answer; even twice, and I will add nothing more'" (Job 40:1-5). God then shows Job more of how little he knows. Job then gives this final answer to God. "'Who is this that hides counsel without knowledge?' Therefore I have declared that which I did not understand, things

too wonderful for me, which I did not know."
(Job 42:3). The idea of us not understanding
what God's ultimate plan is also echoed in the
following verse: "For now we see in a mirror
dimly, but then face to face; now I know in
part; then I shall know fully just as I also have
been fully known" (1 Corinthians 13:12).

God has wonderful plans for us if we follow
Him. In preparing us for these plans, there
is often pain and suffering. Just as plants get
pruned and metal gets refined, so must we
have our "impurities" and "dead branches"
removed. The Bible says "For whom the Lord
loves He reproves, even as a father corrects the
son in whom he delights." (Proverbs 3:12).

It is very clear from the book of Job that God
is in control and deserves to be. When I see
things happening around me that suggest that
God is not in control, such as war, innocent
civilians dying in bombings, children dying
from diseases or starvation, I call back to my
memory that I do not have the wisdom of God.
I accept that He is in fact in control and will
intervene in His perfect timing and perfect
way. I then return to the truth that He is all-
knowing, all-powerful, and all-loving and I am
not. Finally, when I desire to question God's
goodness, I "put my hand over my mouth".

Soli Deo Gloria

More thoughts to come

JULY 23, 2005

The Mosque

Last night as I flew over Baghdad I could see where in the middle of the city the largest mosque in the world is being constructed. This thing is huge. It looks like six large mosques surrounding a huge mosque, but it is just one. Seeing this brings thoughts of freedom and democracy to mind.

Freedom for Iraq is what we say we are here for. People both here and at home often ask what are we really doing here and is what we are doing worth the lives it is costing both us and Iraq? I think this is a very good question.

Fighting for someone else's democracy carries some inherent risks. The main one I think of is that the majority of the people that have been freed from a tyrannical regime may choose to construct and elect a government that seems to us to be no better than the previous bad guys. There is inherent risk in freedom. God knew this when He created us and allowed us the choice whether to follow Him or not. If we look at the new government as a "creation," in a sense, we have also taken a risk. We have American men and women over here risking their lives for a country that may by free election set up a government based on Islam. It is interesting that I would say most of Bush's strongest backers are evangelical Christians who share his belief in Jesus Christ and ultimate worth in people being free.

Unfortunately, the people you make free may choose to build the largest mosque on earth rather than setting a new world record for Vacation Bible School attendance.

As I look to the lessons of history, I think of Japan and Germany. We warred with both of these countries and were involved in their reconstruction. There are many aspects to this comparison that weaken it as a tool to learn from, but we really do not have any other good recent examples. What I am encouraged by as I look at these two countries is to know what they did to their neighbors and even those living within their own borders in the name of nationalistic pride and where they are now. The atrocities of Hitler are well known and Japan is still hated by many of its neighbors for its past evils. That being said, they both are free countries now, which allow people to live vastly different lives and faiths in peace. They also allow people to travel freely both in and out of the country, a hallmark of countries that have little to hide.

As I think of the future of Iraq, what I desire for the country is a life like Germany or Japan. Germany has Christian roots and is largely agnostic now and Japan continues to be a predominantly Buddhist nation; however, Christianity is allowed to be presented in both countries.

Many people are afraid to have other faiths around, especially some Christians. I do not have that fear. I believe that Christianity is the only religion that has the complete truth. Many other faiths have good principles that Christians agree with, but that does not make their whole system true. Jesus said, "the truth will set us free." I believe this is a guiding principle as we present Christianity in the marketplace of belief system options. If it is the ultimate truth that we say it is, then it will stand no matter what persecution may come. The underground church in China is a great example. In fact the church thrives during times of persecution. Now, as we set up our tables in the marketplace, I am well aware that even as the ultimate truth many will still choose not to accept it. **"Enter through the narrow gate. For the gate is wide and the way is broad that leads to destruction, and there are many who enter through it. For the gate is small and the way is narrow that leads to life, and there are a few who find it"** (Matthew 7:13-14). This should not discourage us. Salvation is the work of God, not us. I believe our role is to present the truth in word and deed and let God handle the rest.

So I say let them build their mosque if they like. Give them that freedom. But us being here allows many of us Christians to interact with Iraqis on a daily basis and show them by deed and word that we are not the "Great Satan" that they have been told for so many years but rather the givers of their freedom even at the cost of our own blood. Sounds similar to what Christ did for us, doesn't it? Jesus said, **"The thief comes only to steal and**

kill and destroy; I came that they may have life, and have it abundantly" (John 10:10).

One of my favorite quotes is from the late missionary CT Studd: "Some prefer to live within the sounds of chapel bells, but I prefer to set up a rescue shop within a yard of hell" or, as the case here may be, within 40 miles of the largest mosque in the world.

Soli Deo Gloria

More thoughts to come

JULY 27, 2005

No foot

The other night I was asked to come to the ER to clear a patient for aerovac. As I entered the section of tent that is the emergency room, I could see immediately whom I needed to clear. Lying on an elevated cot, the tent version of a hospital bed, was the wounded warrior. He had multiple injuries and I asked him what had happened. He was very calm as he described the incident that had brought him down this road. He was riding on a helicopter, not inside but on the outside, standing on the narrow piece of metal tubing that is the "landing gear" for this type of helicopter. They were flying very close to rooftops outside of Baghdad and a blanket on a roof was sucked up and somehow wrapped itself around part of the helicopter. The helicopter was momentarily out of control. During this time the warrior fell from the helo and landed on the roof, breaking a leg in numerous places. then as the helicopter spun out of control the tail rotor swung by and cut off the other leg just below the knee. He looked down and couldn't believe that he had lost his foot and knew he needed a tourniquet. He started reaching for his just as his fellow warriors arrived to help with a tourniquet and morphine.

We looked together at the well-bandaged leg. Where there used to be a foot, now there was a stump. He said, "I know I have lost my foot, but I can't look at it right now." I asked if he would like the leg covered with a blanket and he nodded and laid his head back down on the cot. I covered his leg and made sure he was out of pain for the plane ride home.

I know a little of what lies ahead for this wounded warrior. My father lost his arm when I was a boy and I watched as he adjusted. One of the memories that stands out is shortly after he came home from the hospital, we were all at the dinner table and my dad was trying to get a piece of pie out of the pan. As he tried with one hand, the pan just spun not allowing him to remove a slice. Finally, in frustration, he threw the fork at the pie pan.

As I have thought of what lies ahead for the soldier who is returning home less than whole, the book of James comes to mind. Coming home whole is an expression that is near to my heart. My wife has asked me to do that. I hope that I can accomplish what she has asked but much of that is out of my control.

God knows that we are not in control. So how did He encourage us for times when the trials of life seem to overwhelm us? **"Consider it all joy, my brethren, when you encounter trials, knowing that the testing of your faith produces endurance. And let endurance have its perfect result, so that you may be perfect and complete, lacking in nothing"** (James 1:2-4). It is interesting that God encourages us with His eternal perspective. He knows that trials will test our faith in Him. His concern is for us to be complete and to lack nothing. He also promises to be there always: **"'I will never desert you, nor will I ever forsake you', so that we confidently say, the Lord is my helper; I will not be afraid. What will man do to me?"** (Hebrews 13:5-6)

What can man do to me? Well, this soldier had his foot cut off. That is the temporal truth. What I believe that God is most concerned about is the eternal truth of our relationship with Him and where we will spend eternity. If we do not know Him, He is drawing us to Him. Often before we will come to God we need to be at the end of ourselves. We each have our own end of ourselves. For some it is a loss of a family member or friend, for others it is a career, and for still others it is their physical body. I believe God is much less concerned with this soldier's foot than where his spirit will make its eternal home.

If we already know Him, He is refining us. I have felt some of God's refining fire. I feel some now and I know there is much refining yet to be done in my life. God is putting us in the fires to purify us. As gold is heated and reheated it is purified of its impurities. I believe God is preparing us for heaven, through the trials of this earth. **"Endure hardship as discipline; God is treating you as sons. For what son is not disciplined by His Father"** (Hebrews 12:7) New International Version.

That is my perspective on all the tragedy around me. I see it as God either bringing people to a place where they must decide who they are going to put their trust in or He is refining those who are already trusting in Him. This is how I remain cheerful and optimistic looking at the face of a soldier with one less foot. I see a loving God drawing all creation to Himself. Although, I will confess that I look forward to the end of earthly suffering and when **"…God will wipe every tear from their eyes"** (Revelation 7:17).

Soli Deo Gloria

More thoughts to come

JULY 30, 2005

An insurgent hospital?

I was asked to see a 10-year-old Iraqi girl the other day. She had beautiful olive skin, a very delicately thin body, very pretty brown hair and a hole in her chest from a bullet. I was called because she needed an echocardiogram to verify that her heart was not damaged by the insurgent's bullet that had violated her chest.

To see an injured child brought out emotions in all of us working in the hospital that day. What does a situation like this make me think of?

A lot of things!!! Bear with me while I set up some background.

The latest polls state that 61 % of Iraqis believe the country is going in the right direction. 58% of US citizens do not believe there will ever be a democratic Iraq. There are a couple of disconnects in the poll results. One is Iraqis are eyewitnesses, while U.S. citizens are reacting to the news media, which is consistently showcasing the work of the insurgency. The other is that what the U.S. population and what the Iraqis consider the right direction may not be the same thing.

I think what is discouraging the U.S. population is the daily attacks of the insurgents and claims that we are making little headway in improving Iraq. There are some facts surrounding the current conditions in Iraq that are rarely discussed by the media. First of all, there is steady progress in the rebuilding of Iraq: power, water, education, and sewage are all improving. There are two reasons why the improvements are not occurring more quickly: 1) insurgents are purposely targeting projects that improve the quality of the Iraqi's lives, for example, blowing up a water pumping station; and 2) most of the reconstruction plans the U.S. had counted on included the work of non-governmental organizations or NGOs. Many NGOs had lined up to work on everything from medical care to education and were anxious to see the condition of the Iraqi people improve after years of neglect due to war and the greed and corruption of the leaders. As I have flown over Iraq I have seen probably a hundred palaces that are juxtaposed with slums. So what happened to the NGOs? Many have left due to the efforts of the insurgents targeting aid workers. I hope people can see how the insurgents are directly responsible for the lack of the Iraqi's lives improving more quickly. What does the media report? The most recent report I saw was quoting the Council for Foreign Relations and said the U.S. failed to plan for the reconstruction of Iraq. I disagree. What has happened is that the insurgents have been very effective at slowing the reconstruction either directly or indirectly. It appears that they would rather have the Iraqi people poor, sick, uneducated, and under bondage, than free.

I once again ask why aren't the Arab nations condemning the actions of the insurgents? The toll on the U.S. military is really quite small but the effect on the Iraqis is profound. It is clear to those of us here that innocent civilians are getting most of the insurgents' wrath. Where are all of the "peace-loving Muslims"? A recent poll in Britain showed that 25% of the Muslims living in Britain supported the work of the terrorists' efforts in London on 7/7/2005. I do not hear very much from the other 75%. I would imagine that the number supporting the terrorists would be much higher in predominantly Islamic nations.

Why aren't the rich Arab nations working harder to improve the plight of their fellow Arabs since, it seems, they do not want the U.S. or NGOs to do it? The Palestinians in the Gaza strip are a great example of their failure. The living conditions have been described as deplorable. Instead of holding the Arab nations accountable, Israel is often blamed for the living conditions of the Palestinians. The failure of the Arabs to take care of their own has been repeatedly demonstrated since the 1940's and they have been blaming Israel for their failure.

The reason I bring this issue up is because it is part of the history and culture that I believe is driving the current situation. With oil above 50 dollars per barrel many of the Arab nations have had a dramatic increase in their profits. Where do those profits go? In part to palaces and lifestyles that are inconceivable to 99% of the population. Obviously, some make their way to financing the weapons of insurgents, everything from makeshift bombs to bullets, like the one that ripped through the little Iraqi girl's chest and severely damaged her left lung. It is clear that the U.S. cares for the lives of the children of Iraq. We received this girl after the Iraqi hospital didn't feel they could care for her. They knew we would and we could. The Coalition has hospitals that care for U.S. soldiers, insurgents, and innocent civilians just like this precious little girl. I consider it an honor to be allowed to be a part of this girl's care.

As of yet I have not heard of the insurgents opening a hospital to care for all of the innocent people their bombs and bullets have injured.

Soli Deo Gloria

More thoughts to come

AUGUST 4, 2005

Blood type

"There is power, power, wonder-working power, in the blood…"

If you were to walk around this base you would very quickly notice that there is almost an obsession with one's blood type. Some soldiers have it embroidered on their helmets. It is written on some other's nametags. It may be on their uniform and their body armor. It is also found on everyone's dog tags that we all wear faithfully around our necks. Some even place an extra one in a boot just in case. Most of what you see are A+ or O+, the two most common blood types. Every once in a while you will see the precious O-. They are called the universal donors. This blood is coveted for its ability to be given to anyone. It is essential in traumas to keep people alive while the lab is still verifying their blood type and making sure the blood that they are getting, even if it is the same type as theirs, is compatible. The other envied type is AB+. These people are called the universal recipients. It is very clear that the soldiers walking around this base and elsewhere in harm's way want there to be no delay if they ever need blood. They know that there is life in the blood and if they lose too much of this precious fluid their physical body will not survive.

The dog tags are another interesting fact of war. Putting on dog tags to come over to Iraq has a sobering effect (military members typically wear them only when they are deployed). Wearing them causes the realization that I may be in such a condition that I need this tag to speak for me. It has my name, rank, religious preference, social security number and blood type stamped on it. I saw a case that the tag did need to speak for a man. He had been injured by an improvised explosive device (IED). There were hundreds of small injuries on his face. When the bomb exploded, it sent melting pieces of metal everywhere and many had been stopped by his skin, muscle and bone. The injury had caused his whole face to swell. His eyes were closed shut. His lips were three to four times larger than usual. He looked as if someone had beaten his face with a meat-tenderizing mallet, the type with the pointed ends. He would not have been recognizable even to his mother. Seeing him reminded me of the verse that foretold what Christ would look like after he had been tortured: **"Just as many were astonished at you, My people, so His appearance was marred more than any man and His form more than the sons of men."** (Isaiah 52:14). **"But He was pierced through for our transgressions, he was crushed for our iniquities"** (Isaiah 53:5). It hurt me to look at this man. Seeing him in this injured state reminded me of Christ. It reminded me of what Christ went through for my sins.

So how do the blood types and dog tags come together in my thoughts? It is the issue of the blood and needing something to speak for us. It is Christ whose blood can heal us: "**In Him we have redemption through His blood, the forgiveness of trespasses, according to the riches of His grace, which He lavished on us,**" (Ephesians 1:7). And it is Christ who **speaks or intercedes in our defense to God the Father in Heaven: "Therefore He is able to also save forever those who draw near to God through Him, since He always lives to make intercession for them."** (Hebrews 7:25).

When my dog tag was made, I would have preferred for it to say next to blood type: Christ's Blood, since that is the only blood that can truly save me.

Soli Deo Gloria

More thoughts to come

AUGUST 11, 2005

Pity party

It was about 0100 in the morning and I had just finished my workout. I was walking back to my trailer and I was very frustrated at the events of the day. Things happened here, at work back home, and with my medical mission plans for here and Mongolia that all had me frustrated. One of the most difficult aspects about being deployed is that when things happen back home there is often very little you can do about it.

As I left my trailer to go take a shower, I started to have a good old-fashioned pity party. That lasted about ten seconds before one of my favorite sections of scriptures came to mind. The verse comes from the book of Lamentations, which is a perfect place since I was lamenting my current situation.

I first discovered this chapter when I was going through a very difficult time. It was a fiery trial. I can remember reading the third chapter of Lamentations and, as I read, I was agreeing with Jeremiah. I felt my life was horrible and I could identify with these verses: **"My soul has been rejected from peace; I have forgotten happiness. So I say, 'My strength has perished and so has my hope from the Lord.' Remember my affliction and my wandering, the wormwood and the gall. Surely my soul remembers and is bowed down within me."** (Lamentations 3:17-20). These verses rang true to me and then Jeremiah surprised me. Just when we were really feeling sorry for ourselves, he wrote this: **"This I recall to my mind, therefore I have hope. The Lord's lovingkindnesses indeed never cease, for His compassions never fail. They are new every morning; great is Your faithfulness. 'The lord is my portion' says my soul, therefore I have hope in Him'"** (Lamentations 3:21-24). Then, as I read further, more wisdom came: "It is good for a man that he should bear the yoke in his youth. Let him sit alone and be silent since He has laid it on him" (Lamentations 3:27-28). Well, at this point I felt that I obviously had things to complain about, but that God would be there for me. Then came my final lesson from this chapter: "Why should any living mortal or man, offer complaint in view of his sins" (Lamentations 3:39)?

So as I walked to the shower tonight (or actually early this morning) in a lamenting mood, I heard God ask me, "Why should any living man complain in light of his sins?" Immediately I knew what I needed to do. I needed to stop dwelling on what had been frustrating me and, as God said through Paul in the book of Philippians: "Finally brethren, whatever is true, whatever is honorable, whatever is right, whatever is pure, whatever is lovely, whatever is of good repute, if there is any excellence and if anything worthy of praise, dwell on these things….And the God of peace will be with you" (Philippians 4:8-9).

One can imagine there is much to complain about in a combat zone, but my challenge and calling is to find what is true, do what is right, be pure and noble, and encourage love. If I am doing those things, I will have little to complain about.

Soli Deo Gloria

More thoughts to come

AUGUST 12, 2005

God's protection

A couple of recent events here have served to remind me of God's protection. First, let me say that I have been here over three months and our base has received in excess of 120 mortar and rocket attacks; however, less than a handful of people have been injured and none of them seriously.

A few days back a mortar hit a trailer that housed a service member. The mortar came right through the roof and basically demolished the room. It happened at night when the bed should have been occupied, but not this night. This military member has to pull guard duty once a month and this night was his night. The service member in the room next to him (each trailer has three rooms) had a lot of melting hot shrapnel enter his room; however, none hit him. It all hit his mattress instead.

Another recent event also encouraged me as I believe it is evidence of the hand of God protecting us. One of the planes that I fly on pretty regularly was just outside the base and started receiving small arms fire. There were many bullets that came through the fuselage of the plane. One came through underneath the pilot's seat and stuck in the cushion. Another bullet hit right where two people are usually sitting on any other flight but on this day it was just holding a cooler. Another bullet would have surely hit the soldier sitting in a chair,

but his backpack was positioned so it took the
bullet and saved the soldier. Nine bullet holes,
no injuries, and the plane landed safely.

How do I explain this? As I said before, I
believe it is God protecting us. I believe He
is answering the prayers of so many who are
faithfully holding us up before the Father daily.
As it says in Psalm 32:7, which has been made
into a praise song and is a title of an excellent
book: "You are my hiding place; You preserve
me from trouble; You surround me with songs
of deliverance." Another excellent Psalm for
this is Psalm 91: "He who dwells in the shelter
of the Most High will abide in the shadow
of the Almighty. I will say to the Lord, 'My
refuge and my fortress, my God, in whom I
trust'" (Psalm 91:1-2).

Once again, incredible examples of Providence
always beg the question of why do any get
injured or killed at all. First, as I have said
before, I do not pretend to understand the
permissive will of God. The truth of the matter
is that ever since Adam and Eve made their
"big mistake" we live in a fallen or sin-filled
world. Wars are great examples of man's fallen
nature. Greed for power, stature, and money
drive men to do heinous acts to others, even
the apparent innocents of society. However,
God does promise to those that believe that
he will never leave us or forsake us (Hebrews
13:5). He also states through Paul in Romans
8:38-39: "For I am convinced that neither
death nor life, neither angels nor principalities,
nor things present nor things to come, nor

powers, nor height nor depth, nor anything other created thing, will be able to separate us from the love of God that is in Christ Jesus our Lord." From this verse one can see that how God chooses to encourage us is not by saying that we will never die or suffer hardship. He encourages us by teaching that through any trial brought on by anything or anybody, nothing can separate us from His love. His love is obviously more important than our human flesh. His love transcends our physical body. I think we often feel if a Christian dies that is the most horrible thing that could happen. From God's perspective, He is just welcoming a loved one home and into eternal peace and rest. As God says through Paul in the book of Philippians: "For to me, to live is Christ and to die is gain" (Philippians 1:21).

I believe whether we live or die we have God to thank. If we are kept safe from harm, for His protection; if we die, for the joy of joining Him in paradise; and if injured, for the peace of a grace that is sufficient for us. The basic question that comes to mind is, "Do we trust that God loves us, no matter what the circumstance?"

I think it is clear from my writings that I believe in the providential power of God. I do not believe in coincidences and the Bible is full of examples of God directing events for His will to be carried out. The question remains: "Do we trust Him?" I believe if we trust Him we have peace that no mortar can take away

and if we don't trust Him there is no bunker
big enough to calm us.

Soli Deo Gloria

More thoughts to come

AUGUST 27, 2005

Freedom of Speech

I wasn't planning on revisiting this subject,
but a recent discussion with a friend of mine
and what I read in today's *Stars and Stripes*
has motivated me. My friend recently saw the
movie "Monster In-Law" for free at the base
theater. He asked me if I were going to see it. I
told him no because I had no desire to support
Jane Fonda in any way. I do not think he fully
understood my position but a letter to the
editor in today's *Stars and Stripes* puts it very
well.

We have heard that Jane Fonda is planning
a war protest bus tour. This is the majority
of a letter written from a soldier stationed in
Baghdad.

"I'd like Jane to witness Iraqi women
demonstrating for their right to participate in
the drafting of the Iraqi constitution. She could
park her eco-van in front of a local Iraqi father
whose four children were just murdered by
insurgents, or visit the families of Iraqi soldiers
who died fighting for a free Iraq.

She could witness headless bodies of children
floating in the Tigris River and view pictures

of mass graves, one showing a child size
skeleton still clinging to its mother's leg. She
should protest in front of families clawing at
these graves with bare hands, tears streaming
down their weathered cheeks. Tell any of those
people that this war is wrong.

The popular phrase, "I support the troops and
thus I am against the war," is a slap in the
face. It trivializes what we do and suggests
that we are victims. We are not victims! It is
imperative that these terrorists die quickly, and
the troops here are ensuring that happens. We
are proudly serving our country and protecting
our families.

Jane your smile would get you nowhere with
these terrorists. They would call you an infidel,
rape and then brutally murder you. They aim to
do the same to our families. With God's help,
we are the brick wall stopping them. As you
relive your Viet-Nam days, take one second
to think about the Iraqi families who have
suffered so horribly, and understand that there
are men and women daily risking their lives to
ensure this does not happen to you and your
family." Captain Rachel Enicks writing a letter
to the editor in Stars and Stripes

In the same paper there is a survey that shows
people who know someone who has been
to Iraq are much more likely to support the
decision to go to war, approve of the war,
and not subscribe to the notion that the war
has increased the threat of terrorism. It is
interesting that those with a more personal

knowledge of the situation support it more. Knowledge is the key. We hear too much about a few deaths and very little of the increasing rights of women, rebuilt schools, improved water, sewage and electric, etc.

When I hear people like Cindy Sheehan insult our president and ask for an explanation of why we went to war, I would like to remind her of headless children floating in a river and women completely covered in black with a purple finger indicating they had voted for the first time in their lives.

As for Jane Fonda, I will continue to put my self in harm's way to support her freedom of speech. I want nothing less for the Iraqis; neither should she.

A few more thoughts to come

Soli Deo Gloria

SEPTEMBER 2, 2005

The prayer of Wesley

Just before I left for Iraq, an 11-year-old boy named Wesley asked me what he could pray for. I asked him to pray that I would be able to see many Iraqi children who have heart disease and help them to receive cardiac surgery. His mother told me after that, that he prayed every day that my request would be granted. I would like to share the path that God lead me down to answer Wesley's prayer.

Two months prior to leaving for Iraq, I was required to receive training and qualify to use an M-16 in case of emergency. If a doctor is using an M-16 it is a BIG emergency. I met a physician during this training that was going to the same base as I was and she was supposed to work in the ICU. I told her I would see here there. During my time at my base, I had a few requests to screen children in Iraq with heart problems but I was only allowed to see a few due to safety concerns. I also never saw the doctor I had met. I just assumed that she did not deploy. Well, about six weeks ago, I was in Baghdad and eating at one of Saddam's old palaces, which had been converted into a cafeteria for deployed troops, and I ran into the doctor who I met during my training. She ended up deploying as the Physician Liaison to the Iraqi Air Force Surgeon General. We exchanged pleasantries and I thought nothing more about it.

About two weeks later I received an e-mail that went out to a large number of pediatric cardiologists worldwide, asking if there were any military pediatric cardiologists in Iraq. I responded to the e-mail and said I was in Iraq and would be willing to help if I could. The person who had asked was the director of a non-governmental organization called www. shevet.org. It is a Christian organization that works to obtain care for Iraqi children who need heart surgery. They have already helped fifty Iraqi children to receive cardiac surgery in Jordan, Israel, Europe and the US. Imagine this: an Iraqi child is helped by a Christian organization to get life saving heart surgery in Israel. Only the hand of God can work those types of miracles. The director of the NGO contacted a physician at the Ministry of Health for Iraq. I contacted the doctor I did M-16 training with to see if evaluating Iraqi children would be something that the Iraqi Air Force Surgeon General would support.

After a about a hundred e-mails, the screening was approved. I went to Baghdad and set up a portable clinic in the National Iraqi Assistance Center. I was able to evaluate 57 Iraqi children with complex heart disease in two days. Most of the children were blue because of a lack of oxygen in their blood due to defects in their heart. Of the fifty-seven, forty-seven need surgery. Twenty-seven of the forty-seven do not need any more tests and can be sent for care as soon as arrangements are made. The remaining twenty need additional studies before they will be ready for surgery. Eight children were not candidates for surgery due to the severity of their disease and delay in treatment. Two children were in good health and had only minor heart defects that did not need surgery.

Over and over again the Iraqis were very thankful for what was being done for them and stated they did not want the U.S. to leave. They felt that we were the only ones helping them. They wanted to reassure me that there are only a minority of people who are violent and most want peace and democracy. There were two school age boys who, unprompted, said to us, "Bush" and gave the thumbs up sign.

It was an incredible opportunity for me to show these children and their families that the U.S. cared for them and it was all brought about because of God answering the prayers of an eleven-year-old boy named Wesley.

Thank you, Wesley. "...The effective prayer of a righteous man can accomplish much" (James 5 16b).

Please join me in prayer for these children and their families.

Soli Deo Gloria

One more thought to come

SEPTEMBER 5, 2005

FINAL THOUGHT

There are a couple of different ways of getting home from Iraq. Most leave via large charter aircraft. I was able to fly home a different way as a flight surgeon. A patient who had had a little too much of combat needed a medical attendant to accompany him on the aerovac flight to Germany in case he decompensated on the plane and required medication. I was chosen to care for this tired soldier on his way to Germany and then I would catch a cargo plane home. The flight to Germany was uneventful and the patient did well. When I arrived in Germany I found a plane that was going to Dover Air Force Base in Delaware. I had about 16 hours between landing and my next flight. When it was time for me to board the aircraft, I assembled all of my gear, which was two large gear bags each weighing about 75 pounds, an echocardiography machine, and my personal belongings. I was at the base of a ladder that led to the crew compartment of the C-5 that was to carry me back to my home, the U.S.A. I started to carry the first oversized bag up the ladder. I needed to climb about 15 feet to the door. As my eyes cleared the door I saw who was joining me on my flight home. In the front of this huge cargo plane, sitting very stately on a pallet, was a flag-draped casket. It took my breath away. My traveling partner and I were at the two extremes of coming home. I was looking forward to waving the flag and he was under the flag. My eyes teared as I took in the sight and the difference of our fates. The base I was at took over 150 mortar and rocket attacks during my four months. Any one of those mortars could have hit me and some came very close, but I was spared any injury. Instead I returned home in better shape than I have been for a long time.

The flight to Dover lasted about nine hours. As soon as we landed the honor guard appeared to take the fallen soldier from the plane. The C-5 has a unique feature. Because it is so tall in order to load or unload cargo the front of the plane can be lowered. When the plane does this it is referred to as "kneeling". In order for the flag-draped casket to be removed from this plane, it would need to kneel. It seems fitting for such a solemn event that even the plane would kneel in reverence for the sacrifice of the fallen. As the door of the C-5 opened there was the honor guard, called to attention by their leader. I was excited to be back home; in contrast, the honor guard was somber as they performed the duty of honoring the fallen Marine. What a contrast indeed! Two members of the armed services were coming home. I walked with a renewed energy in my step even though it was after 1:00 am. The Marine was carried for transport to a waiting family and his final resting place.

I had hoped to be home on the 3rd of September. It was what my wife, many friends and family members had been praying for. Before I saw my fellow passenger on the C-5, I did not understand why God had chosen the delay. However, when my eyes saw the mourning flag, crisply tied to a stainless steel casket, I started to understand. God had taught me much during my four months in Iraq. He had taken care of me and my family. He had showed me the bravery of young men and women, and He had helped me to understand what my father-in-law went through during Viet Nam. I witnessed the very best and worst of what man can do. I saw people literally blown up and I saw people risking and sacrificing their lives for others. I saw a people encouraged by the hope of freedom and a life free of tyranny. I saw Iraqi children playing with toys donated from people who had never met them and probably never will, in hopes of bringing joy and a smile to a face that had seen the horrors of war and an insurgency bent on stealing the freedom that was won with precious lives.

As I end my "Thoughts from the Cradle" I want to share with you what I feel God taught me. It comes from a song that He used to challenge and sustain me through difficult times.

All I once held dear, built my life upon
All this world reveres, and wars to own
All I once thought gain, I have counted loss
Spent and worthless now, compared to this

Now my heart's desire, is to know You more

To be found in You, and known as Yours

To possess by faith, what I could not earn

All surpassing gift of righteousness

Oh to know the power of Your risen life

And to know You in Your sufferings

To become like You in Your death my Lord

So with You to live and never die

Knowing You, Jesus, knowing You

There is no greater thing

You're my all, You're the best

You're my joy, my righteousness

And I love You Lord

I have no higher thoughts.

Soli Deo Gloria

VOLUME II: JANUARY 2007- MAY 2007

DUKE IS BACK IN IRAQ - 1/18/07

Well folks, my great friend and the Godfather of my children has been called back to Iraq. Here's his first entry:

JANUARY 18, 2007

Going back

When I wrote my last Thoughts from the Cradle in September 2005, I did not intend for there to be any more. I felt God had given me insights during a certain time and that time had gone. However, now I am back in Iraq and I am overwhelmed with thoughts from this "Cradle of Civilization".

My main job at home is to treat children with heart defects. When I deploy, I go primarily as a flight surgeon. My other skills of pediatrics and cardiology are used as needed. I have been sent to Balad Air Base in Iraq to serve both rolls. I will act as a flight surgeon, keeping fliers healthy and clearing the injured for aeromedical transport, and as a pediatrician, caring for Iraqi children who are injured and brought to our hospital who require critical care skills.

I left my home on the 14th of January and the U.S. on the 15th of January. I arrived in Iraq on the 18th. Leaving home for the second time was much harder than the first for me, my wife, and the rest of my family. The first time I didn't know what to expect. What was it like to be gone for 4 months? How often would I get to talk with my wife and my son? Would I be in danger? Now, I know and knowing made parting with my wife much more painful for both of us. As I thought of leaving, I was reminded of another great parting. This parting was not for months and was not even a parting of people. The parting I am thinking of and was reminded of during Christmas was when Jesus Christ left heaven and came to earth as a baby. He left the unspeakable comforts of heaven and came to our world. He left the constant fellowship with His father. He voluntarily and temporarily set aside many of His attributes as God to walk our earth in our vulnerable flesh. He left knowing that he was going to be in danger. He even knew how long he would be here and could foresee what His future held and still He came. When we as deployed service members leave our homes and feel loneliness, despair, and miss our families and comforts of home we are in good company. Jesus Christ, the creator of the Universe, has done the same.

Then there was The Almighty God, the Heavenly Father, who sent His son. For the families who are the senders; you have had to part with your husbands, wives, sons, daughters, moms and dads. The good news is you are in great company. The Almighty God knows what it is like. He sent His Son into a world that was much less comfortable than Heaven, knowing that His Son would eventually suffer an excruciatingly painful death to atone for our sins. God is not a God who is far off. He is a God who is familiar with sending and being sent. He knows what it is like to give so that others may have life and that abundantly.

What an incredible plan of Jesus Christ and His Father to have gone through what we have gone through, so when we pray and cry out for help, we know we have a heavenly Father who is familiar with our state and can gently and lovingly reassure us: **"And He has said to me, 'My grace is sufficient for thee: for power is perfected in weakness.' Most gladly therefore will I rather boast about my weaknesses, so**

that the power of Christ may dwell in me."
(2 Corinthians 12:9).

I will dedicate "Thoughts from the Cradle, Volume 2" to a dear friend, Lt. Col. Mark Murphy. I met him in Iraq in 2005. He was like a brother to me and encouraged me as I wrote 42 "Thoughts" last time. He died shortly after returning home, but now is in his eternal home. I miss him.

My name is Kirk Milhoan. I sign as Duke, a call sign, in memory of the surfing pioneer Duke Kahanamoku and the beautiful beaches of Hawaii. I long for the day to once again be on a beautiful beach with my wife. There is a lot of sand here, but no beaches or surf and definitely no wife.

More thoughts to come

Soli Deo Gloria

Duke

JANUARY 20, 2007

In December 2006, Al Gore, former Vice President of the United States of America, was quoted extensively when he called the Iraq war the "worst strategic mistake in the history of the United States". Let me now take you to January 16, 2007. On this day I boarded a chartered DC-10 that was taking about 190 of us Air Force members to Qatar and then, for most, on to Iraq. We were all leaving the comforts of home and our families. We were

not sure we would come back. We left because
it was our duty. Our Commander-in-Chief
had sent us so we were on our way. When we
arrived in Bangor, Maine for a fuel stop, the
first person I saw, as I exited the plane, was an
elderly gentleman proudly sporting a World
War II veteran cap. He shook everyone's hand
that walked off that plane. He was not alone.
There were many other Veterans of Foreign
Wars, as well as other well-wishers without
hats. They shook everyone's hand and then
applauded. They thanked us for our service to
our country and wished us well. They had cell
phones for anyone who needed to call family
and had a shop dedicated to commemorating
what soldiers had done filled with snacks and
treats. The greeters shared their stories and
wanted to hear ours. When we returned to the
plane, they all lined up again and wished us
well and shook all of our hands. It was after
midnight before we left. The last person to
greet us was the World War II veteran. Imagine
if you were leaving your family and friends
and the comfort and safety of home. As you are
preparing to leave you hear that you are about
to be engaged in the "worst strategic mistake in
the history of the United States". How would
that make you feel about the sacrifice you were
about to make? I would imagine just about
everyone reading this would say it would make
it much more difficult. Earlier, Senator Kerry
accused the military of terrorizing Iraqi women
and children in their homes. To say that you
support the troops but do not support the war is
meaningless drivel. Those comments showed

absolutely no support for what the armed forces is doing and makes us feel as what we are sacrificing and dying for is a useless campaign.

In 2005 I wrote about a Patriot Detail where we honor the fallen as their flag-draped casket is loaded on the plane for the trip home. I was able to go to one such detail during my four-month tour. The name of the service member was Specialist Travis Andersen. As I looked at the items the greeters had in front of their store, I saw a large three-ring binder. I was curious to see what it contained. I thought it was probably pictures that service members had given; instead it was the names of all of the fallen. I turned a few pages and then found the name I knew. My eyes teared as I thought of the day when his flag-draped casket passed by and I rendered a very slow and somber salute. The greeters knew what it was like to fight for freedom and have lost friends who had given it all. They knew how painful it was to remember the horror of war and live with the memories of: sights, sounds and smells that would never go away. The greeters supported us and we felt it. The handshake and the kind words of the World War II veteran made me deem irrelevant the careless and callous thoughts of men without honor.

Politics stops at the water's edge, especially when U.S. service members are in harm's way.

More thoughts to come

Soli Deo Gloria

JANUARY 23, 2007

I have been thinking a lot about the depth of emotions lately. You can imagine with saying goodbye to my wife and caring for the injured and dealing with those who have died or are dying, I am living in a sea of emotions.

One of my favorite war movies is "We Were Soldiers". The reason is, in part, due to the way the film handles the families who are left behind and must come to grips with the injury or death of a loved one. There is a scene, at the end of the movie, when the doorbell rings at the house of Lt. Col. Hal Moore. It is late at night and his wife looks out the window to see who is there. What she sees is a yellow cab, the exact type that delivers telegrams notifying the wives that their husbands have died in battle. She starts to cry and demands that the children go upstairs. She opens the door only to find her husband standing at the door. Her emotions pour forth as she is transformed from a grieving spouse to a celebrating wife.

My wife and I enjoy watching "Extreme Makeover Home Edition". In this reality show, ABC picks a family who has had an enormous tragedy and completely renovates their home. There are always tears on both sides of the TV as those who had almost nothing are given just about everything they could ask for. If it were not for their desperate state, the height of emotion would not be there. Imagine Donald Trump receiving a 3000 square foot home in middle America, with a 32-inch plasma TV, custom kitchen, bedrooms, and bath and a pool. I doubt that he would cry with joy.

I think that there is a limit to how positive our emotions can be; however, I do not think there is any limit to how bad things can get. Imagine the worst thing that you could think happening to you. For a service member it is probably being captured and held like those in the Hanoi Hilton. Little food, beatings, sickness, loneliness, isolation; but then there is always a chance that someone could come and stick a needle in your eye and make it worse. What I am trying to say is that the height of the emotion is dependent on how bad things were or are and not on how good things become. I think about my goodbye with my wife. The tears come from not only the thought of separation for 4 months but for the very real possibility that I may not return. The closer I am to harm's way, the greater the depth of the emotion when I return. This holds true when someone who is not expected to graduate college, or make the pros, or survive cancer, makes it through triumphantly. We love those stories. I dream about the day when I get to see my wife in the airport on my arrival. The harder and more dangerous it gets over here the greater it will be to arrive safely home to her warm embrace. Jesus talks about this in a sense when he is speaking about those who have lived horribly sinful lives and then have been forgiven by His grace and live victorious lives through the power of the Holy Spirit.: **"For this reason I say to you, her sins, which are many, have been forgiven; for she loved much. But he** who is forgiven little, loves little" (Luke 7:47). The depth of the transformation is what makes them love Him more than others who have been forgiven of less.

It is so nice to fantasize about the emotional highs, the stories that are made into movies. As I watch those movies, I often desire to have that kind of emotional high, but what I have realized and question more recently is whether I really want to go through the low of fear, loneliness, financial, physical, emotional and spiritual torment that make a story worthy of a movie. Sometimes we don't have a choice and it is the life we have been given.

The next time you see someone in a military uniform come off a plane and see the family come running to them with tears in their eyes and hold onto them and never want to let them go again, appreciate how low it must have been for that family and rejoice with them now…it might be me and my wife.

"Rejoice with those who rejoice; and weep with those who weep" (Romans 12:15).

More thoughts to come

Soli Deo Gloria

JANUARY 25, 2007

Before we departed the U.S., when we arrived in Qatar, and then again three more times when we arrived in Iraq, we were all told about General Order 1 A. It is the special regulation relating to our behavior while we are in the AOR (area of responsibility). The basic idea of this order is to keep people acting appropriately in a combat area. The orders include: no gambling, no cohabitating with the opposite sex, no alcohol, no pornography, no drug use, no going into mosques unless escorted by a Muslim, no bringing in personal weapons, no attending host nation executions. Then there is one that reminds me of Sesame Street's "one of these things is not like the other." General Order 1A j: "No proselytizing or attempting to win converts to any religion, faith, or practice." I thought about this last one when I was doing my daily Bible reading. I was reading in the book of Matthew: **"And blessed is he who does not take offense at Me."** (Matthew 11:6).

In the last couple of years there has been quite a bit in the news about sharing one's faith in the military, especially in the Air Force. There was a scandal at the Air Force Academy because of sharing faith. There has been a recent change that chaplains can no longer pray in Jesus Christ's name at official events, but only during private ceremonies, such as funerals. The last few years you have seen more and more "Happy Holidays" and less and less "Merry Christmas". Interestingly, a recent poll performed by Zogby showed that more people were offended by "Happy Holidays" than by "Merry Christmas". There have been some great books written on the subject: "The Name" by Franklin Graham and "The Trouble with Jesus" by Joseph Stowell, to name a couple. These books deal with the war against Jesus. In our society, even as it is acceptable to talk about God and spirituality, Jesus is becoming increasingly off limits. It is almost always because of evangelical Christians sharing their faith that issues arise. People are offended by people talking about Jesus, praying to Him in public, and sharing what He has done for them and what He has to offer. Most of the people who are offended have probably not read Matthew. If we are not offended by Jesus, then we are blessed. I doubt that the offended people realize that their offense that seems so noble and so pluralistic is actually keeping them from a blessing.

I sense that the blessings of God are slowly being removed from the U.S. and I think it is in part due to the offense people feel toward His Son, Jesus. I am in the military and have taken an oath to follow my leaders. So what does a person who has a belief system that at the very core calls me to share the good news of the Gospel of Jesus Christ do in such a situation? In words attributed to St. Francis of Assisi, I will "Preach the gospel at all times and if absolutely necessary use words." In 1 Peter 2: 12 it states, **"Keep your behavior excellent among the Gentiles, so that in the thing in which they slander you as evildoers, they may, because of your good deeds, as they observe them, glorify God the a day of visitation."** And later in Peter he continues to encourage us: "Who is there to harm you if you prove zealous for what is good? But even if you should suffer for righteousness, you are blessed. And do not fear their intimidation, and do not be troubled, but sanctify Christ as Lord in your hearts, always be ready to make a defense to everyone who asks you to give an account for the hope that is in you, yet with gentleness and reverence" (1 Peter 3:13-15).

So do I have a problem with General Order 1A? Not really. I do not believe that I can "win converts" to Christ. That is the work of the Holy Spirit. My challenge is to be a light that shines hope and be ready to give an accounting of where that hope comes from.

More thoughts to come

Soli Deo Gloria

JANUARY 27, 2007

I get pretty weary of American citizens or our allies referring to George W. Bush as a terrorist. He is not a perfect man and he has made mistakes. I wonder if anyone could tell me of a man or president who hasn't. Consider the leaders during WWII, the Korean War or the Vietnam War. In retrospect, mistakes were made, but that is part of war and it is aptly stated that "hindsight is 20/20."

I wanted to go through my last four days and use what my days consisted of to dispel this notion once and for all that the Commander-in-Chief or the military members who serve under him are terrorists.

Earlier in the week, I was asked to write the death certificates for some military members whose helicopter went down. It was not easy and as I was going about the task, my thoughts went immediately to families who were grieving. This was also sobering for me as I have flown many times in the very helicopter that crashed and it was not difficult to see myself in their position. The next couple of days were spent clearing injured patients for aerovac. This is a 24/7 job. There are always helicopters coming and going; planes coming and going; patients being loaded and unloaded; techs, nurses, and docs caring for these wounded warriors. In addition, we are the place where the locals will bring their children and family members for care when they need it. In the past four days, I have been involved in the care of two children who have been struck by IEDs and were brought to our facility for care. I have also been involved in caring for two children who had head trauma following car accidents and one child last night who fell into a BBQ and severely burned her face, hands and knees. We had another young child who was shot through the buttocks and leg by a sniper. When I was helping one child the father came up to me and thanked me and looked up to the heavens and gave thanks as well. I do not think he thought of me as a terrorist. If your child were injured, you would not bring them to a terrorist or "The Great Satan" for medical care. The Iraqis appreciate the care they receive from us and hope and pray for more. I am just one doc retelling a four-day period. Consider how many docs we have and how long we have been here doing the very same thing. That is one of the reasons why the Iraqis will often plead with us not to leave. I have heard them say, "Please do not leave us."

That brings me to last night. I finished my 16-hour shift clearing patients at 7 a.m. I went back to my trailer and got about 4-5 hours of sleep. After lunch, I went to write some e-mails and my commander stated that he needed me to transport a detainee to the hospital where detainees are cared for. This patient was on a ventilator. He was on a ventilator because he received quite a bit of trauma after he and his two buddies were caught by an attack helicopter setting an IED. He survived; his accomplices did not. After the incident he was picked up by a medevac helicopter and brought to us for care. He received excellent care and will likely survive. This type of activity surely does not sound like the work of a group whose commander is a terrorist. This is a story of a group of armed service members who do not take war as a personal vendetta but rather a profession of arms.

As the nurses, techs and I prepared him for transport, one of the docs came up and in frustration stated that he wish he had just died. I understand that emotion. We see a lot of service members and civilians who have been injured, maimed, and killed by IEDs. A lot of resources were going to be used to care for this man who hours before was trying to

kill us. I didn't respond to him, just nodded
with understanding and thought about a higher
calling. Jesus told us: "**Truly I say to you,
to the extent that you did it to one of these
brothers of Mine, even the least of them, you
do it to me**" (Matthew 25:40). I think this man
qualified as the very least of my brethren. So as
I struggle with the emotions of it all, I imagine
this is Christ that I am caring for. And I try, but
fail often, to "**do your work heartily, as for the
Lord, rather than for men**" (Colossians 3:23).

I hope everyone can see the compassion of
the troops, who are following the lead of their
Commander-in-Chief. He is no terrorist.

Soli Deo Gloria

More thoughts to come

JANUARY 28, 2007

Unity

Today in *Stars and Stripes* is a short article
about General Lynch, who is in command
of the Army's 3rd Infantry Division that
will be directly affected by Bush's plan for
more troops. It stated that the General had
said "…war-weary Americans should 'quit
complaining' and prepare themselves for the
conflict to continue several more years." He
went on, "I believe it is time for us to quit
complaining and focus on our duty." Lynch
said it is not soldiers and their spouses who are
complaining about the war, but rather people
in "outside circles" from the military." He

then added, "If we let the American people realize…that historically it takes at lest nine years to complete a counterinsurgency operation, then the American people will be supportive."

I recently read about another famous battle in history. It is recorded in the book of Exodus. It is the battle of the Nation of Israel against the Amalekites (Exodus 17:10-13): "**Joshua did as Moses told him and fought against Amalek; and Moses, Aaron and Hur went up to the top of the hill. So it came about when Moses held his hand up, that Israel prevailed, and when he let his hand down, Amalek prevailed. But Moses' hands were heavy. Then they took a stone and put it under him, and he sat on it; and Aaron and Hur supported his hands, one on one side and one on the other. Thus his hands were steady until the sun set. So Joshua overwhelmed Amalek and his people with the edge of the sword.**"

It is interesting that nothing is said about whether the plan was correct or if the troop numbers were right or if Joshua were a good leader, but only the need for Moses to keep his hands up. The only thing that was important in this battle was Moses to show a sign of strength and keep his hands up. When he grew weary he needed people to come alongside and help him to maintain the appearance of strength even when he was exhausted. When I read this story a few days ago, I immediately thought this was a beautiful example of what is happening in our struggle. The Amalekites

could probably see when Moses grew weak
and were encouraged, but when his friends
realized that he needed support and joined
in, Joshua and his army prevailed. Right now
there are protests in the U.S. Capitol. They
are in essence pulling down the hands of the
Commander-in-Chief. The protests are telling
the insurgents that the troops here are not
supported. Thus, the terrorists and the countries
that support them are empowered and trust that
they just have to keep up the small menace of
killing a few here and there and wait for us to
quit.

I am not prepared to quit and turn this country
over to people who do not care whether
innocent women and children live or die and
think nothing of sacrificing them in open
markets and streets.

The media has weakened our leader at home
and abroad. Someone needs to grab a stone for
him to sit on and some others need to grab his
arms and support him. All of us down on the
battlefield will continue to fight and care for
the injured but we need the country to be "one
nation, under God, indivisible, with liberty and
justice for all." Sound familiar???

Soli Deo Gloria

More thoughts to come

FEBRUARY 1, 2007

The Media

The other night we had a call that an urgent patient was coming in from an outside base and was going immediately to surgery. We met the patient at the flight line. We backed our ambulance up to tail of the C-130, engines running. We boarded the aircraft to get the patient, a Marine, who was intubated (breathing tube inserted) because of his level of consciousness. The flight nurse and his buddy, another Marine, were taking turns bagging (breathing for) the injured Marine. We transferred the Marine to the ambulance and drove to the hospital. I took over the bagging while we traveled. As we got out of the ambulance and entered the ER, the docs, nurses, and tech were all waiting and descended on the injured like a group of mother hens all eager to help. I continued to bag as they set up the ventilator. There was a bright light in the ER that night. It was a TV camera. There was a film crew from one of the networks who wanted to document what we did. They like to follow a patient all the way along the process: point of injury (almost never done, haven't seen a film crew on a helicopter going to the scene of a newly wounded soldier), medevac (helicopter), surgery and stabilization, staging for aerovac (CASF), and then the aerovac to Germany and eventually home. This is done quite a lot. While I was here last time, we had at least four different crews doing just what I had described. They

usually just stay at the Green Zone and Balad
and do not go out into the field.

It is very flattering to have cameras around
and have the press wanting to interview you,
but as I was bagging the Marine and I saw
the bright lights I had another thought. It goes
back to one of my favorite movies, "When We
Were Soldiers." The reason there is a movie
is because there was a journalist who risked
his life to document the incredible feat it was
to take the "hill." When the battle was over, a
helicopter landed and a lot more press jumped
out in safety and wanted to tell the story. What
they saw were all of the dead and injured,
but that was not the story. The story was the
bravery that caused the death and the injuries.

Showing what the medical people do in a
war is in a very real sense showing defeat.
Concentrating on the wounded and how
the wounded are cared for is very nice, but
nonetheless focuses the light on us and the
wounded and not on the true heroes. Yes, we
work hard and have an incredible track record:
96% of people who make it to our hospital
survive to make it home. Our motto is "We
bust ours to save yours" and it is true. The
medics keep the hospital open 24 hours a day 7
days a week with no slow down for weekends
or holidays. It is easy to lose track of what day
of the week it is because, except for church on
Sunday, everything else is the same.

But, back to the my concern about the
publicity we receive, constantly showcasing

the wounded and the deaths with the steady death count that is constantly spoken of on TV and printed in everything from local papers to the *Stars and Stripes* emphasizes the tragedy of a conflict without the balance of what has been gained. When was the last time you heard a news account about the number of girls in school, how well the Kurds are running their provinces, the freedom people have to disagree without the threat of their families being murdered? How about the young girls who are no longer used by Saddam's sons and then tossed aside? What about all the medical care that is given to men, women and children who are injured in normal traffic accidents? The cameras did not spend any time filming all of the humanitarian care we are giving. What about all of the heroism, when men jump on grenades to save their buddies? Most of the reporting from here is done from the safety of a base like Balad or from the Green Zone. Laura Ingraham tried to talk about this when she was interviewed on NBC after traveling outside of the Green Zone and no one wanted to let her give her viewpoint.

The media seems so compassionate when they are filming the hospital but I doubt the purity of their motives and I long to hear the real story told by a reporter who is brave enough to stand side by side with the real heroes of this conflict, the soldiers and Marines on the ground.

Soli Deo Gloria

More thoughts to come

FEBRUARY 3, 2007

Heroes

They recently replaced a flag at the hospital. It lines the underside of a covering that the injured pass through as they come off the helicopters to enter the hospital. The flag is very large. I would say it is around 12 by 20 feet. It is majestic and glorious. The covering is aptly named "Heroes Highway." The injured often come on stretchers on their backs and, if they are able, they can see the flag welcome them to the hospital. The walking wounded limp beneath its protection.

The U.S. flag is an incredible symbol. I have one in my room that was with me during my last tour. I know this may sound strange but as a kid if I could have been an inanimate object it would have been the U.S. flag. I remember being at a Lakers basketball game and everyone standing in respect as it waved so proudly as the National Anthem played. I recently saw the movie "Flags of Our Fathers". This movie is about the flag that was raised in Iwo Jima. The battle for Iwo Jima, which took weeks, was very difficult and much more costly in lives than this current struggles has been in years. When the first flag was raised on top of that hard fought for hill, it buoyed the spirits of the men and they celebrated. The movie then spent the rest of the time showing how the military was making heroes out of some of the men who were there that day and using them as a way to sell war bonds. The men, some of who were not or did not feel like heroes, tried to get this point across again and again, but without success.

As I watched the movie I started to think about what makes a true hero. I believe the word has been so overused in our society that it has lost much of its meaning. We often call the military, police, coast guard and firefighters heroes. Why? I believe the common thread is that they all risk their lives for others. Some of those they are trying to save would not extend them the same effort. Jesus said, **"Greater love hath no obe than this, that one lay down his life for his friends" (John 15:13). As I thought about this more, I realized the hero is demonstrating the greatest type of love and the reason we hold these people up and even idolize them is because they have put into human action what many of** us would like to be able to give but have failed to show to even our most loved. When people are in the presence of a hero there is a natural desire to stand to honor them.

There is a desire in our hearts to do a heroic act that is there because Jesus Christ is calling us to do what He did when He laid down His life for us, so that we may live, not only on earth but also for eternity. Jesus gave us the example of what it means to be a hero. Imagine how many lives He has saved and will save from sin, despair, heartache, loneliness, and eternal separation from God, for any who will believe in Him.

The other night we had a very injured soldier come into the hospital. He was rushed to the operating room and the doctors, nurses, and techs worked valiantly, but they were unable to save his life. His injuries were too great. This death devastated the staff. As they lifted the lifeless body off of the operating room table and carried him away, the entire operating room stood at attention. Why? Because when we are in the presence of true heroes it is a natural desire to stand to honor them.

Soli Deo Gloria

More thoughts to come

FEBRUARY 9, 2007

It seems that almost every city in Iraq that is the midst of a conflict is called a Holy City. The day when there is violence there is often called a Holy Day. What you do not hear a lot of is any challenge to what made this day or city holy and if there are any means of supporting such a claim. The Buddhists made large statues in Afghanistan and considered them holy and then the Taliban came and tore them down. When my wife and I were in Tibet, there were temples that were considered holy and the Tibetans would travel hundreds of miles on foot as a pilgrimage to the holy site. Recently in the news there is debate over rebuilding a ramp to the Temple Mount in Jerusalem. The Jews consider this site holy because it is the place where the Temple was built. The Muslims believe this place is holy because this was where Mohammed went up to heaven.

In our post-modern world and belief system it seems that many people believe in one God who just has been given many different names. I had one of the airmen I am deployed with state that it doesn't matter what you believe as long as you believe in something. This is a difficult time for many of us who grew up with absolutes: truth and lies, good and evil, right and wrong. The truth is that there cannot be a place that is holy to one religious group and considered worthy of being destroyed by another group if we all believe in the same God just with different names. Christians believe that, as Jesus said, "I am the way, and the truth, and the life; no one comes to the Father but through Me (John 14:6). And "For God so loved the world, that He gave His only begotten Son, that whoever believes in Him shall not perish, but have eternal life" (John 3:16). "For by grace you have been saved through faith, and that not from yourselves; it is the gift of God; not as aq result of works, so that no one can boast" (Ephesians 2:8-9). This belief system is at odds with Hinduism, Buddhism, and Islam. When we all meet the Almighty God, some of us are going to be right and some of us are going to be wrong.

This idea of people feeling that they are just as holy as anyone else is not new and, in fact, Moses had to deal with this very issue. Starting in Numbers 16:3-5: "They assembled together against Moses and Aaron, and said to them, 'You have gone far enough, for all of the congregation are holy, every one of them, Everyone in the entire community is holy, and the Lord is among them, and the Lord is in their midst, so why do you exalt yourself above the assembly of the Lord?' When Moses heard this, he fell on his face; and he spoke to Korah and all of his company, saying, 'Tomorrow morning the Lord will show who is His, and who is holy, and will bring him near to Himself.'" In the morning they both presented themselves and this is what God said to Moses (Numbers 16:21): "Separate yourselves from among this congregation, that I may consume them instantly." It didn't matter how strongly Korath believed he was holy; what mattered was what was the truth. The truth is set by God and, whether we agree or not, it is still the truth. The truth in this story was that Moses was chosen by God and Korath was not. It was a lie for Korath to think that he stood in the same position as Moses did before God.

We find ourselves in a similar situation in the world today. The war on terror is a war of ideologies. One ideology is to make the whole world your convert and have every nation fly an Islamic flag. The other ideology is to allow people the freedom to choose what they believe. The latter is the exact paradigm God has given us. He has presented His Son as a sacrifice for us, but has not forced us to believe. When Jesus met people he did not force them to follow Him. He simply showed them signs of His Godly power and then gave them the option whether they would choose the

145

broad road that led to destruction or the narrow road that led to eternal life. It was their choice.

The Bible talks about a day in the future just like the day Moses had thousands of years ago (Matt 25:31-34,41): "But when the Son of Man comes in His glory, and all the angels with Him, then He will sit on His glorious throne. All of the nations will be gathered before Him, and He will separate them one from another, as the Shepherd separates the sheep from the goats; and He will put the sheep on His right, and the goats on the left. Then the King will say to those on His right, 'Come, you who are blessed of My Father, inherit the kingdom prepared for you from the foundation of the world.'.... Then He will say to those on His left, 'Depart from Me, accursed ones, into the eternal fire which has been prepared for the Devil and his angels.'"

No matter what people, the media, or books say, there is truth and lies, good and evil, right and wrong, heaven and hell. There is one Holy God and we need to be on the right side...with the sheep.

Soli Deo Gloria

More thoughts to come

FEBRUARY 11, 2007

Soul scrape

There is a certain purity in ignorance. When we are faced with a problem, if all we know

is the problem then our concentration can
be focused on the problem and solving the
problem. The more extraneous details we are
given, the more complicated and confusing a
given situation may become. I have thought
of this principle a lot as I see the surgeons
operating on patients. The patients they operate
on come in a variety of types. There is the
wounded American soldier, innocent civilian,
coalition force soldier, civilian contactor, Iraqi
soldier, or even terrorist, who may be Iraqi,
Iranian, Syrian, or another nationality trying
to further destabilize the region. The operating
room is set up to have two operations going
on in the same room. At times it has had an
armed forces member on one of the tables and
a terrorist on the other. You can imagine how
hard this can be for a surgeon and the staff who
have been up all night, thinking here they are
away from their family, missing anniversaries,
birthdays, and graduations, to be busting theirs
to save a guy who hours before was trying to
kill "us". There are a couple of ideals at work
here. One is simply the professionalism of
doctoring. Once the drapes go on the patient,
faces aren't seen and stories aren't told; there's
just bleeding that needs to be stopped, broken
bones needing to be fixated, organs that need
repair, and so on. The purity of ignorance is
that once the drape is over the patient, the
blood of child-adult, soldier-civilian, hero-
terrorist, Iraqi-American all looks the same.
There is a problem to be solved, the drapes
cover the faces, and stories are usually quiet
during anesthesia. However, there is a story

that comes in with the patient and there is a
time when the drapes are not covering the
faces. Side by side, there is a soldier who was
blown up by an IED and a terrorist who was
found setting the IED and was blown up by
a rocket or missile fired by those trying to
protect and give freedom to the fledgling Iraqi
nation. How do these doctors deal with this?
Part is summed up by a quote from Abraham
Lincoln that is written on the plywood wall of
the tent where the surgeons rest between cases:
"With malice toward none, with charity for
all…let us strive….to care for him who shall
have bore the battle."

A friend of mine, who is one of the surgeons,
and I were talking last night. I was seeing him
off as he was returning home for a short time
to bury his father who had died suddenly. We
talked of what we have seen and the pain of
caring for bodies burned, broken, crushed and
mangled. We didn't talk about which bodies,
just the bodies we see regularly. I shared with
him how I felt just before coming back to Iraq.
I was at an Air Force training for operating in
a field hospital. During one of the lectures for
the doctors we were reviewing procedures for
handling severe trauma and there were many
pictures. The pictures immediately brought me
back to Iraq, even though I was in the middle
of San Antonio. As I watched the slides, I
said to myself, "I do not want to see any more
blown up bodies." When I came back from
my first tour here I asked my wife if Iraq
had changed me. I didn't really feel changed
but just wanted to see what she thought. She

said, "You don't let the little things bother you as much as you used to." As I continued to watch the horrific slides, I realized I had been changed and had become much more sensitive to the trauma of war. It was no longer just a Hollywood movie with gory scenes as the slides brought back real memories of the injured, dying and dead.

As I go about my daily duties here, I do not think I am much different than when I am at home. I still laugh and say a lot of silly stuff, but today at church I noticed I cry easily. Because at the very heart of the matter this warrior is really just a child and needs time to jump up on Daddy's lap and allow him to put ointment on my scrapes and sores. The scrapes and sores are on my soul and I do not ever expect them to be completely healed until heaven. This is probably one of things about war that those who have been a part of it can never really explain to those who haven't. It's not because we don't want to. It is simply because it is hard to describe what it is like to have your soul scraped.

Soli Deo Gloria

More thoughts to come

FEBRUARY 23, 2007

Over the span of 5 days, I was in Iraq; Kuwait City, Kuwait; Dubai, United Arab Emirates; Addis Ababa, Ethiopia; Djibouti; and, finally, Sana'a, Yemen. Traveling like this has allowed me to see many different cultures in a very

short amount of time. I also had a chance to
read many different newspapers and to watch
news from a variety of sources, including an
English version of Al Jazerra.

One of the most easily recognized differences
is the dress. Throughout my travels, I saw
everything from the most conservative dress,
the burqa, to some of the most revealing
outfits designed being worn in the same public
spaces. The differences appeared to blend into
a fabric of multicultural dress and seemed to
be at peace with each other. I realized I do
not find the conservative dress of many of
the women in the Middle East as offensive as
much of what I see in Europe and the U.S. I
do not think the modest female is such a bad
thing when compared to the other extreme,
such as those who wear very short skirts
and do not seem to care about underwear.
The conservative dress can be criticized for
preventing a woman from expressing herself,
but in this culture that is not always something
that is desired. I once was performing an
echocardiogram on a Yemeni girl of 12. She
felt great shame for having a man see her even
partially uncovered. It is true that the more
conservative dress leaves less temptation for
men, as opposed to much of the West where
hardly anything is left to the imagination.

But enough of the dress; I was much more
interested in what I read in the Kuwaiti
Newspaper. There was a long article on how
Kuwait and Saudi Arabia were discussing
with the Iranian government how to bring Iran

into a modern approach to Islam and not to
continue to follow a traditional old-fashioned
view, which includes violence and suicide
bombing.

After Kuwait, my next stop was Dubai. The
headline on their English language newspaper
there was "U.S. plans to attack Iran by the
spring." Dubai is an interesting place because
it seems to be all about consumerism and
making money. The United Arab Emirates
(UAE) have the best hotels, biggest mall,
and largest indoor ski slope, and have made
islands shaped like the globe and a palm tree
to increase waterfront property. Their airport
is a living entity at all hours of the night and
prides itself on having the most duty-free
shopping of any airport in the world. Kuwait,
Bahrain, and UAE share many similarities; the
two most striking are incredible wealth and
a relative peace compared to their neighbors.
Iraq has more oil, better land, and currently a
huge military presence, but very little signs of
wealth or peace. So what is the difference? I
see two separate problems with Iraq right now:
sectarian violence that took off one year ago
after the bombing of the third holiest Shiite
shrine in Samarra likely by Sunni's and, maybe
more importantly, Iran destabilizing the area
by sending in militants and weapons. In the
Middle East there seems to be a choice that is
separating the governments: material wealth
vs. radical Muslim beliefs. I am not a great fan
of absurd material wealth, but it is definitely
easier to travel through a nation that wants
your money rather than your neck.

I bring this up in the context of the U.S. Congress wanting us out of Iraq regardless of the security situation. It reminds me of other great conflicts where the people lost heart in the midst of a battle. It started with the nation of Israel not finishing the job God had given them to clear out the Promised Land before them after crossing the Jordan. Instead, to this day, they still live with enemies surrounding them. Others that come to mind: World War I and Germany returning just a few years later to fight again; World War II and Russia, that Patton wanted to conquer but instead we had years of Cold War; Korean War and North Korea; Iran taking our hostages and Carter's ineffectiveness; and Desert Storm and failing to defeat Saddam at that time. There is a long history of paying a costly price for losing heart in the middle of a battle.

A big division is occurring in the world. With rare exception, the world does not want to follow the U.S. They want the U.N. to lead. It is globalism vs. nationalism. I heard Bette Middler once say that the hardest thing about being successful is finding someone who is genuinely happy for you. The U.S. is suffering from the same attitude around the world. Like a little kid, the world is saying "you aren't the boss of me". But who will be the moral leader, if not the U.S.? The U.N. has shown itself to be all talk and little action even when, for example, millions are dying in Sudan.

Recently there have been bombs in Pakistan, India, and Malaysia. The U.S. does not have

a presence there, but still suicide attacks
continue everywhere. The time we are in is
historic. Ideologies are at war and it is not for
the faint of heart. God told Joshua after he had
already promised the land to the Israelites,
**"Then you shall return to your own land, and
possess that which Moses the servant of the
Lord gave you beyond the Jordan toward the
sunrise."** (Joshua 1:15)." Interestingly, God
didn't say it was going to be easy. He said
that **Joshua** and Israel as a nation were going
to need to be committed to the path God was
sending them on. The President said to us as
we started the global war on terror that it was
going to be long and difficult. The U.S. public
is losing heart, and the strength and courage
they displayed immediately after 9/11 is
waning. If this strategy of Iran's is successful,
it will continue beyond the cradle and I have
no doubt violence and death will once again hit
our homeland. Many don't remember, in the
1970s, how horrible it was to hear every night
on the news how many days Iran had been
holding the hostages at the U.S. Embassy. Can
we afford to allow Iran off the hook again as it
wages a secret war against the U.S. disguised
as an insurgency?

I am currently in a nation that has an official
state religion, which is not very friendly to
other beliefs. The clerics that are pushing much
of the efforts to destabilize Iraq have said they
will not be satisfied until there is an Islamic
flag over every nation. Joshua found the people
of Israel at a crossroads as well and gave this
challenge: **"Now, therefore, fear the Lord and**

serve Him in sincerity and truth; and put away
the gods which your fathers served beyond the
{Euphrates} River [Iraq] and in Egypt, and
serve the Lord. If it disagreeable in your sight
to serve the Lord, choose for yourselves today
whom you will serve; whether the gods your
fathers served which were beyond the River,
or the gods of the Amorites in whose land you
are living. But as for me and my house, we will
serve the Lord (Joshua 24:14-15)."

Soli Deo Gloria

More thoughts to come

MARCH 3, 2007

Every so often, we have explosions on the
base. When I was last here we had 152 in 120
days. They are usually mortars or rockets.
Fortunately they rarely cause any harm to us
because the base is so large. They actually do
cause a fair amount of porta-potty damage. The
other night there were quite a few explosions.
It made me think of the National Anthem and
the portion: "And the rockets red glare, the
bombs bursting in air." The "Star-Spangled
Banner" can be hummed by most, some can
recite the words, and fewer yet can sing it well.
However, what I have been thinking about is
what the second verse has to say. Here it is:

O thus be it ever when free men shall stand

Between their loved homes and the wars
desolation;

Blest the victory and peace, may the heaven-
rescued land

Praise the Power that has made and preserved
us a nation.

Then conquer we must, when our cause it is
just,

And this be our motto, "In God is our trust";

And the Star-Spangled Banner in triumph shall
wave

O'er the land of the free and the home of the
brave.

This is just a very small part of our very strong
religious history. I am saddened by how often
the strength of the conviction of our forefathers
is minimized by revisionist history. The
importance of the faith of a nation at war is
clear from the second verse. The first tells us
that the banner standing is an encouragement;
the second tells us who deserves the credit.

Just like in the days of Francis Scott Key, Iraq
has had its fare share of explosions, bombs
and rockets. The other night on this base they
"gave proof through the night that our flag[s]
were still there." Here, the Iraqi and the U.S.
flags fly beside one another and the colors (red,
white, and blue) do not run.

Soli Deo Gloria

More thoughts to come

MARCH 4, 2007

As I was walking along today, I thought about a principle I learned in my surgery rotation as a medical student. For people who have signs and symptoms consistent with an acute appendicitis, the appropriate next step is to take them to surgery for an appendectomy. It was taught and expected that there will be a certain number of people who go to surgery who end up not having appendicitis. In fact, the expectation was that a surgeon should have around 5% of the cases taken for an appendectomy be normal, or else his index of suspicion is not high enough. The principle is that it is better to take out a normal appendix than to wait until an inflamed one ruptures and increases the risk of infection and death.

This same principle applies to national security. I have heard many complain that no weapons of mass destruction (WMDs) have been found in Iraq, so we are not justified to be here and, for that reason, we should pull out and President Bush should be impeached for lying to the Congress and the American people. Let me set the record straight with completely de-classified information that anyone could find if they looked hard enough (a challenge to reporters).

There have been over 500 weapons of mass destruction found in Iraq since we invaded, and this is just the unclassified information. The weapons contained at least two different types of chemicals, both nerve and blister

agents. The criticism and explanation why
this information does not get bigger press is
that these were old weapons and not evidence
of a new weapons program. That, however,
does not negate the fact that Sadaam was in
possession of WMDs and could have used
them against Iraqis or others. Another piece
of information is that a gas lab was found
in northern Iraq that had new materials for
making blister and nerve agents. These
materials would have been obtained during
the time Sadaam was saying he did not have
an active chemical weapons production
program. A last piece of information is that
there are people who are Syrian and are
testifying publicly of three places in Syria
where WMDs from Iraq were hidden and are
still there to this day.

We all look at our surroundings through our
own biases. I look at my surrounding through
the eyes of a Christian and a physician. The
way I view these events in Iraq which have
and continue to directly affect me and my
family, friends, and co-workers is that when
there is a real concern the U.S. must take
action to protect its citizens. On rare occasions
the U.S. has over-reached, which, back to my
analogy, verifies that we have a high index
of suspicion; however, usually, we are late,
when the pus has already started leaking into a
country. There are numerous countries around
the world that we have not invaded, because
they posed little or no risk to the U.S. or our
allies' interests. Before invading Iraq, this
country showed many signs and symptoms

of a weapons program that could have had a devastating effect on the world. Like the surgeon, the U.S. decided to act and operate. I do not have the entire operative report but what I have found is that during the first part of the operation, there was "old pus found in the belly." If old pus is left in the belly of a human, it will fester and eventually come to light when the patient is much more sick and much harder to treat. The treatment for pus in the belly is drainage of the pus and to make sure there isn't any more pus around. Additionally, one must look for where the pus was coming from and stop its production. We are still in the midst of the operation and we are still looking for more pus and different types of pus.

Where this illustration breaks down is when a doctor is operating on a patient the concerned friends and family are in the waiting room thinking and praying for the patient and the doctor. I have been in operations where the families patiently waited most of the day for news of the results of the operation. In this conflict the neighbors are adding pus to the already sickened body and some of the so-called friends and families of the doctor are ridiculing the result before the operation is complete, having grown weary of waiting.

My recommendation as a physician is to trust those who are in the operating room and see firsthand how the operation is preceding, rather than those who are in the waiting room and want to go home regardless of whether the patients lives or dies.

Soli Deo Gloria

More thoughts to come

MARCH 8, 2007

I was reading the *Stars and Stripes* the other day and saw an article that said a recent poll showed that only 28% of American's thought we would win the war in Iraq. I found this very interesting considering I had watched the movie "The Green Berets" the other day and was amazed by some of the similarities of the issues facing the Green Berets and what we are facing today during the global war on terror (GWOT). It was also interesting to think of what movies Hollywood was producing during the Viet Nam War compared to now.

First, I thought I should address the issue of when people use the words "winning the war in Iraq," the words they should really use are "winning the global war on terror". The war in Iraq has been won. The Iraqi government and the U.S. government are not at war. We are in Iraq at the request of the elected government. We are no longer at war with Iraq. We are still at war with terrorists who are largely targeting fellow Muslims in Iraq. That is to say the war we are fighting in Iraq is the global war on terror. This should be shouted from the rooftops because what we are seeing and hearing from the world media is the viewpoint that we have already lost and the coalition should pack up and leave.

During the first part of "The Green Berets," there are a couple of sergeants who are talking with the media and showing how incredibly smart and well trained the Green Berets are for the conflict in Viet Nam. The program is very impressive, but at the end a reporter says: "My paper does not support the war. Tell me why we should still be fighting in Viet Nam?" The sergeants go on to explain all of the tragedies that were being carried out on the innocent civilians in Viet Nam and how the U.S. needed to be there to protect the innocent. A sergeant then asks the reporter if he had ever been to Viet Nam. The reporter answered with a sheepish "no". This movie was made in 1968 and President Lyndon Johnson was asked and allowed Hollywood to shoot many of the scenes with military equipment. This was during the height of the war and almost the exact same questions were being asked of the military by the media that are being asked today. The conversation is almost identical. If the military were asked "why we are here?", we would answer that "many civilians are being killed." And if we the military asked the media and talking heads in Washington "have you been there, on the ground, outside the wire?", most would have to answer "no".

I have come to believe that it is not the Commander-in-Chief that gets us into a "quagmire," but rather the media that start to call it a quagmire and continue calling it a quagmire until the people believe them. By not reporting the facts but rather presenting analysis, the press they weaken the public's resolve and ultimately decrease the worth of the sacrifice made by the soldiers. Being a hero or getting a Purple Heart in a war that is considered a losing cause diminishes the perception of the honor of the act no matter what people may say otherwise. The soldiers of Viet Nam fought just as hard if not harder than those of WWII, but they do not get the title of "the greatest generation."

Let me give you some numbers from previous battles. I will provide the link in case people want to study these numbers: www. en.wikipedia.org/wiki/Death_toll. WWI: 8,500,000 military deaths; WWII: 24,456,700 military deaths (418,000 U.S.); Korean War: 36,516 U.S. deaths; Viet Nam: 58,209 U.S. deaths; GWOT: around 2,600 U.S. deaths so far from combat. Can you imagine if the U.S. media reported the Battle of the Bulge or The Battle for Iwo Jima like it reports battles today? What about D-Day? Surely if Roosevelt and Truman had the current media or even the media from the Viet Nam days there would have been calls for their impeachment. If it weren't for the steadfast resolve of the U.S., the national language of France and Great Britain would be German, and Japan would own all of Hawaii. One can see how few we have lost in Iraq, after years of fighting terrorists in difficult street battles and booby-trapped roads. Imagine what today's press would have called D-Day.

As expected in "The Green Berets," when the reporter went to Viet Nam and saw what the soldiers were doing his mind slowly began to open and see the war from a different side.

As I look back at what I have written so far during this tour, I see a stark contrast from what I wrote during my last tour. During my last tour I spent a lot of time talking about the bravery and sacrifice of military members. Most of what is on my mind now and what I write about is trying to help people to see that the cause we are engaged in here is just and honorable. I hope that this will be my last "thought" on why what the military is doing here is working, is not a quagmire, and is worthy of honor for the troops involved. I hope to return to writing about the heroism, bravery and sacrifice of the incredible men and women of the armed forces that I have the privilege of caring for.

The American public was patient during WWII, when 1,000,000 were injured and half that died. When 9,000,000 had died by 1916 and it seemed that WWI would be lost or seemed at least impossible to win, no one gave up because the stakes were too high. The stakes are even higher today, as it seems like madmen are procreating at an alarming rate. We must not lose our resolve. The war we are fighting is global.

It looked grim when Jesus was crucified. His disciples lost their resolve and fled. Then 50 days later the Spirit of God descended and the world was changed forever. The press is saying that evil has won in Iraq and it is useless to continue fighting. They have reported negative stories until the public has lost their resolve and are encouraging us to flee. I am willing to stay as long as I must. I continue to trust that in the end good will conquer evil and that the Almighty, who sees all and is ultimately in control of all, is still on His Throne.

Soli Deo Gloria

More thoughts to come

MARCH 11, 2007

Heroism

I have been thinking about three words lately and those are: courage, bravery, and heroism. It seems like they are often used interchangeably, but as I went to the dictionary for a precise definition I received an education. As I thought about these words, I thought courage was a willingness to be brave and bravery was when you really had to come through when things were scary or going very badly. Here are the actual definitions:

Courage: The ability to face danger, difficulty, uncertainty, or pain without being overcome by fear or being deflected from a chosen course of action.

Bravery: Extreme courage in the face of danger or difficulty.

Hero: Remarkably brave person.

I learned that the words are a hierarchy, which makes their use not interchangeable at all but rather degrees that must be assessed by someone. There is a hierarchy in the military as well. There are those who do not deploy; those who deploy to safe areas that could be in danger; those who deploy to areas of danger and get bombed; those who walk the streets of the bad areas protecting the innocents; and those who go out looking for bad guys. For civilians, those in the military are often called our nation's heroes. For us in the military many of us do not feel like heroes. We have not done anything "remarkably brave". Those who have to deploy and still carry out their jobs while bombs, mortars or rockets are falling would fit the criteria of having "courage". I think this is where I would fit in. I recently received an e-mail from my older brother. He said "glad to hear that you're not going up in the copters too much. One combat medal is enough, don't you think?" The combat medal he is referring to is a medal I received for aerial flight during combat during my first tour. It is a medal that requires acts of courage from the recipient. Flying in helicopters or airplanes that could be shot at is considered courageous, so that is why I received it once I had done this at least 20 times. My reply to him will require some explanation. My reply was "Yeah, one combat medal is enough. Bravery and heroism are over-rated as a volunteer. It is another thing if it is thrust upon you." I wrote this before I knew the exact definitions, but I think even then that I knew there was a difference

between being courageous and being brave
or a hero. I can elect to be courageous and go
into harm's way. I can continue caring for a
person during an "alarm red", when mortars
and rockets are coming into the base. I can
volunteer for that level of courage. I think
bravery and heroism is a much more difficult
decision and has fewer volunteers. Courage of
the level I have written about seems tolerable
for me. For some, it might not be; for others,
the activities I am involved in might not seem
courageous at all. However, to take what I am
doing and raise that to the level of extreme
courage, that is a level most do not want to
be involved in, much less raise your hand and
step forward to be involved in. These are often
the tough decisions commanders make when
they have to choose which men are going out
on dangerous assignments. When God was
picking warriors, he had people who were
afraid go home. We have the same system, in a
sense, in our all-volunteer military. Those who
are too afraid do not have to join.

One can see that if brave is extremely
courageous and a hero is a remarkably brave
person, then a hero has extremely remarkable
courage. I thought of one such person today.
This is a man who knew he had an assignment
to do but even to the last moment was seeing
if he could get out of it. He had volunteered
but as the time got closer to becoming a hero,
the task loomed larger and the reality of the act
he was going to perform was becoming truly
daunting. The man became so stressed over
the act he was going to be asked to undertake

that he started sweating drops of blood, which can happen under episodes of extreme stress. The place this event occurred was the Garden of Gethsemane, the man who had to make a choice was Jesus Christ, the task He had before him was to take all of the punishment for my sins. He could have chosen not to do it. He could have chosen to have thousands of angels come and take him away. He prayed to his **Father, "My Father, if it is possible, let this cup pass from Me; yet not as I will, but as You will." (Matthew 26:39) Earlier, I wrote about a hero being** a person who is willing to die for another. People often ask me why I love Jesus so much. Have you ever seen how a person feels about the one who gave their life so the survivor could live? Jesus died for me so that I could live for eternity. He had a choice: take all of the ridicule, pain and suffering of a horrible death of crucifixion for me or go back to heaven knowing I would never be there. It is humbling to know that He loves me more than I ever love him. He is my true hero. On the cross He demonstrated extremely remarkable courage and one more thing: love.

Soli Deo Gloria

More thoughts to come

MARCH 16, 2007

No more questions

I was clearing a patient for aero-evacuation the other day and witnessed a very touching scene. A soldier, who had been hit by an improvised explosive device (IED), was lying in bed, his face severely broken and bruised, his ear drum ruptured, and his eyes barely able to be opened, but tears rolled down his face as the chaplain held his hand and encouraged him. The chaplain held his hand for over 5 minutes as he ministered to this troubled soldier. I am not sure what the discussion was, but the main reason that soldiers cry after they have been injured is because they will not be able to return to their unit and they will leave their buddies behind. The other reason I have seen soldiers cry after injuries is the question "Why me?".

In a trauma hospital where one sees the injured day after day, it is common to hear people ask, "What is the purpose of all of this?". When people see apparent injustices, a common statement is "When I get to heaven, I have a lot of questions for God." It is interesting that Jesus specifically addresses this very statement. Jesus encourages us with this: **"Truly, truly, I say to you will weep and lament, but the world will rejoice. You will grieve, but your grief will be turned into joy. Whenever a woman is in labor she has pain because her hour has come. But when she gives birth to the child, she no longer remembers the anguish because of the joy that a child has been born into the world. Therefore you too have grief now, but I will see you again and your hearts will rejoice, and no one will take your joy away. In that day you will not question Me about anything (John 16:20-23)."** Jesus uses the birth analogy elsewhere when he is describing the earth before the "Great Tribulation": "But all of these things are merely the beginning of birth pains (Matthew 24:8)." I think the reason people want to ask God questions is that they doubt whether He is truly loving. It is common to hear people ask, "If God is such a loving God, then why is there all of this suffering?". Jesus' response is simple. When you finally see Him, you will not have any questions. It will be absolutely clear that He is all-knowing, all-powerful, and all-loving.

The other reason people often do not trust Jesus is because they feel that He has not answered their prayers. You can imagine how many prayers are being said by soldiers when they are in harm's way. The feeling is that when they needed Him most, He was not there. Just a few verses later in John 16 you see Jesus explaining why prayers are not always answered the way we want them. He states, "Until now you have asked nothing in My name. Ask and you will receive, that your joy may be made full." (John 16:24) The condition is that your prayers will be answered by God in order for your joy to be made complete. God is drawing us to Him or refining us once we are already following Him. He is not concerned with answering prayers for our partial joy or fleeting joy. He is concerned with our joy being complete. When those who have believed in Him and see Him after all of our sorrows in this temporal life, our joy will be truly complete and there will be no questions, just worship.

I am very thankful for people who will hold
the hands of those who are hurting and comfort
those who cry until we see Jesus face to face.
**"And He will wipe away every tear from their
eyes; and there will no longer be any death;
there will no longer be any mourning or crying,
or pain: the first things have passed away."**
(Rev 21:4)

Soli Deo Gloria

More thoughts to come

MARCH 20, 2007

We have a variety of alarms here at the base,
which tell us what to do when we are being
attacked or have been attacked. When we
are in "Green", everything is good. We are
not being attacked currently or, if we have
been recently attacked, we are now safe to
continue about our normal routine. "Alarm
Yellow" is after an attack when we have to
make sure the base is safe and that there are
not any unexploded ordinances (UXOs). We
must remain under cover at this time unless
we are on a team that searches for UXOs.
Once "All Clear" is called we are then back to
Green. "Alarm Red" is sounded when we are
under attack. During this time we are to take
cover and remain under cover until "Alarm
Yellow" is sounded. The "Alarm Red" siren
is a little disconcerting; however, what really
gets your attention is when over the loud
speakers you hear "INCOMING, INCOMING,
INCOMING." This means that the attack is

in your immediate vicinity. What we have to
do in this situation is drop to the ground and
cover our eyes, ears, and head as best as we
can. At this point you wait for the proverbial
other shoe to drop. These episodes generate
a lot of thoughts, as you can imagine, but the
one that came to my mind the other day is that
there is a word that is used sometimes in the
U.S. that can generate the exact same reaction
from people. People will become frightened,
flee the area, or just cover their eyes and ears
until the threat is gone. What word could strike
such fear in people? What could possibly send
people fleeing when they live in the safety
of the U.S.? The word has two syllables. It
is a simple name. It just happens to be the
"Name above all names."(Ephesians 1:21)
New International Version It is the name
that at the end of time every knee will bow
to and every tongue confess that He is Lord
(Philippians 2:10-11). It is the only name that
has the promise of salvation: "And there is
salvation in no one else, for there is no other
name under heaven that has been given among
men by which we must be saved." (Acts
4:12) The very scary word is: Jesus. We are
usually not scared of those sent to save us
from destruction. When we are in a burning
house, a fireman is welcome. When our house
is being robbed, a policeman is a welcomed.
When people in the Old West were frightened,
knowing the U.S. Cavalry was coming buoyed
their spirits. Isaiah 9:6 describes the man
who carries this name: Wonderful Counselor,

Mighty God, Eternal Father, Prince of Peace. These attributes do not sound very scary.

There are members of my own family that consider any discussion of Jesus tantamount to hearing "INCOMING, INCOMING, INCOMING." Jesus knew this and talked about it when he described what belief in Him could do to a family. "Do you suppose I came to grant peace on earth? I tell you, no, but rather division; for from now on, five members in one household will be divided: three against two, and two against three. They will be divided, father against son and son against father, mother against daughter and daughter against mother, mother-in-law against daughter-in-law and daughter-in-law against her mother-in-law (Luke 12:51-53)." He also knew that belief in Him would lead to others hating you. "...you will be hated by all because of My name (Matthew 10:21b)." Jesus said to expect it if you were a follower of Him. A lot of people can talk about spirituality or God today but few will allow Jesus to enter their conversation except in vain. Even Christians find themselves walking carefully when they are referring to their Savior. They can call him God, for He is, but to call him Jesus acknowledges who their Savior is.

On a military base, especially in Iraq, there are a lot of very harsh words used. Curse words are used frequently and in a number of very creative ways: nouns, verbs, adjectives, adverbs, commas, objects, indirect objects, etc. Most people will hear these words that not too long ago would have quieted a room, and continue with their work without giving the incredibly foul language a second thought. However, I say Jesus at the same level but in a reverent way and the room will become silent and you can feel the tension rise.

If, as you read this you start to feel tension rise, what has happened is that the Mighty God is now speaking over the loud speaker of your heart and, instead of the frightful "INCOMING" that I hear on this air base in Iraq, The Prince of Peace is asking a question, "AM I COMING IN?". **"Behold, I stand at the door and knock; if anyone hears My voice and opens the door, I will come in to him and dine with him, and he with Me. He who overcomes, I will grant him the right to sit with Me on My throne, as I also overcame and sat down with My Father on His throne."** (Revelations 3:20-21)

Soli Deo Gloria

More thoughts to come

MARCH 22, 2007

I just recently watched the movie "300". I do not recommend it because of its gore and demonstration of the sexual perversion of the King of Persia, Xerxes, but it was a great story of honor, bravery, integrity and self-sacrifice. There are other movies that have similar character values highlighted and are widely popular, like The Patriot, Blackhawk Down, Saving Private Ryan, We Were Soldiers,

Gladiator, Braveheart and The Passion to
name just a few. What these movies all have
in common is men fighting wars against
tyranny with the main character demonstrating
the previously mentioned highly regarded
character traits. These movies are all very
violent and show men at their worst and at
their best, which is required. To show the men
of ultimate honor they must be counterpoised
with how badly men can act. Wars and killings
are usually a common theme.

I thought about the idea of the honor of
men being highlighted at their most trying
moments as I was reading the account of the
first Christian martyr, Stephen, in the book of
Acts. There is a poignant passage as he was at
the end of his trial and was about to be stoned.
**"But being full of the Holy Spirit, he gazed
intently into heaven and saw the glory of God,
and Jesus standing at the right hand of God,
and he said, 'Behold, I see the heavens opened
and the Son of Man standing at the right hand
of God!'" (Acts 7:55-56) Skip a few verses
and you hear Stephen's last words. "They went
on stoning Stephen as he called on the Lord
and said, "Lord Jesus, receive my spirit!' Then
falling on his knees, he cried out with a loud
voice, 'Lord, do not this sin against them!'
Having said this, he fell asleep." (Acts 7:59-60)**

It is interesting that Stephen's death and final
words were very similar to those of the Lord
Jesus to whom he was going. They both died
a very painful death. Two of the very last
statements of Jesus are: **"Father forgive them**

for they do not know what they are doing"
(Luke 23:34) and "....Father, into your hands I
commit My spirit." (Luke 23:46b)."

As I look at the main characters of the men
represented in the Biblical accounts as well as
the movies there is a common theme.

300: King Leonidas and his 299 men fought
against a million men and remained brave
and steadfast in their commitment to defend
freedom even if it meant their death.

Gladiator: Maximus was betrayed and his
wife and son killed. He died by treachery as
he fought for the freedom of Rome from the
tyranny of the Caesar.

Blackhawk Down: Two Snipers remain on
the ground voluntarily while people are being
evacuated and voluntarily give their life so
others can live. The two snipers ultimately die.
Interestingly, "So others may live" is the motto
of the Combat Search and Rescue Squadron.

Braveheart: Wallace fought against the tyranny
of the British Empire for freedom for Scotland
and died crying out "Freedom".

The Patriot: Benjamin Martin loses two sons as
he fights for the freedom of the colonies.

We Were Soldiers: Lt. Col. Hal Moore
demonstrates the utmost bravery as he and his
men fight against incredible odds to secure a
mountain in a conflict to keep free the South
Vietnamese.

Saving Private Ryan: Captain Miller gives his life and the lives of many of his men so one man can return home.

Stephen: He dies for his uncompromising beliefs in the Lordship of Jesus Christ. As he is dying he demonstrates no malice towards his killers, but rather asks for their forgiveness.

The Passion: Jesus represents the ultimate example of the best of men. He temporarily leaves heaven to come give His life through a brutal death so those who believe in Him can be with Him for all eternity. As He is being tortured, He has the opportunity to call for help, but He doesn't say a word, even as He is mocked. If He had been rescued we would not have a Savior.

The stories of the men and movies that depict their acts are very inspiring to many others and me. I am daily talking to men who have risked their lives for the freedom of others and many have lost friends while fighting against tyranny and terror.

As much as I admire these qualities, they come with a price. To show great integrity, there must be great temptation to be dishonest. To demonstrate bravery, there must be a high likelihood of death and fear that would paralyze most. To be considered self-sacrificial, you must be willing to give up what is rightly yours even if it means you go without or even die. To have honor that separates you from others, you must have faced the most severe difficulties and remained true to ideals of honesty, selflessness, forgiveness, mercy and a willingness to give your life for others.

The other aspect that should not be overlooked is perspective. Stephen knew what He was dying for. He was dying for pronouncing the truth about freedom through Christ. When men know they are fighting for freedom from tyranny, the very nobility of their charge elevates their character. There is no meaning to the height of character without the balance of the depth of treachery that it must overcome. When I dissect it to its most basic element, it seems that, using Jesus as the example, freedom is what is most important. **"Jesus said to him, 'I am the way, and the truth, and the life. No one comes to the Father but through me" (John 14:6) He also said, "If you continue in My word, then you are truly My disciples; you will know the truth, and the truth will make you free." (John 8:32) He has set us free from the wages of sin ["For the wages of sin is death, but the free gift of God is eternal life in Christ Jesus our Lord."](Romans 6:23) by sacrificing himself, being put to shame, dying an agonizing death, and remaining silent while he was punished for our crimes. He voluntarily "took the bullet" for us.**

The Soldiers, Sailors, Marines and Airmen in Iraq and Afghanistan are risking their lives for the freedom of others. I would hope the fallen are remembered as demonstrating what is best in men and die with the knowledge that they will be regarded as men worthy of great epic stories.

Soli Deo Gloria

More thoughts to come

MARCH 26, 2007

A couple of days ago, I was walking into the hospital just as a helicopter was arriving with an injured soldier. When they take the injured off the helicopter they place them on a rolling stretcher. The man was being rolled through "Hero's Highway" as he passed by me. He was wrapped in a mylar blanket which helps keep the injured warm. There was a splint around his lower leg, which was wrapped in an Ace bandage, and just his toes and top part of his foot was visible. His foot was blue due to a tourniquet that had been placed to stop the bleeding from a wound further up his leg. Every second or so, blood would drop from the splint, leaving a trail of blood splattered on the ground every six feet as the stretcher rolled into the ER where the orthopedic surgeons were waiting. He would then be prepped for surgery and taken to the OR and the damaged leg repaired. From the foot's standpoint, it only knew it was in pain and was not getting enough of what it needed or wanted. The foot, if it could think independently, would probably be shouting, "How about some blood down here?" "Don't you see my foot is blue?" "I am in pain. I am throbbing. I feel my skin is about to burst. Can I get some relief?" If the foot were given immediate relief and the tourniquet was released, the foot would be happy for a short while. Then, as the body continued to lose blood, it would become cold and blue once more and then would die, as would the rest of the body to which it is attached. As I watched this soldier roll past me I thought, "There is a lesson in what I am seeing." It was 1 a.m. the other morning when I realized the lesson from the "the blue foot".

The blue foot couldn't see the bleeding from its vantage point. It didn't know that the body was at risk of bleeding to death. It didn't realize that the tourniquet that was causing all of its complaints was actually saving the foot in the long run. The foot did not have the perspective that the medic did when the tourniquet was placed. The medic didn't ask the permission of the foot, but just did what was best for the body, knowing that saving the body was the only chance to save the leg and the foot.

The collective church is referred to as the "body of Christ". As I thought about the foot being indignant as to how it was being treated and neglected, my mind went immediately to my prayers as a "foot". There have been times when I have cried out in pain, whether physical, spiritual or emotional, and have wondered why my requests were being neglected. As I look back, when I have cried out because of how unfairly I felt I was being treated, was my life really being saved and was there a tourniquet on another part of the "body of Christ" that caused me pain but would ultimately make me better? The blue foot has reminded me of a very important lesson that I seem to need to learn over and over again. God sometimes puts a tourniquet on a leg. He knows the injury and sees the bleeding that I don't see as the foot. **"For my thoughts are not your thoughts, nor are your ways My ways." Declares the Lord." (Isaiah 55:8) "There is a way which seems right to a man [or foot], but its end is the way of death (Proverbs 16:25)."**

When you are a foot and the Medic is putting a tourniquet on the leg, listen to the Medic and you will **hear "Be still and know that I am God." (Psalm 46:10) New International Version**

Soli Deo Gloria

More thoughts to come

MARCH 31, 2007

I wanted to describe a place and situation and see what comes to mind. The place I am thinking about is surrounded by a fence with razor wire on top. The guards around the fence are armed and can shoot anyone who attempts to go through the fence. Those who are on the inside are not allowed to leave unless the authorities say it is OK. They are housed at no cost to themselves. They receive plenty of food. They are told what to wear and when they can wear it. They are also told how and when they can exercise. They are allowed certain magazines and programs but are not allowed to have alcohol and drugs, although some bring it in illegally. They are told that they are there for a certain time and can expect to be released at the end of their time, but sometimes, due to circumstances, they are kept for longer periods. There are dangers to being in this place and many of the occupants are capable of killing. What does this sound like? Some might think what I am describing is a prison. It is actually a military base in a deployed location. The main difference is that the occupants of the military base have volunteered to be considered for such duty. In the case of the national guard and reservists, many have left jobs back home and come, setting aside many freedoms to serve their country.

I thought of the analogy to prison as I was considering the remarkable stories of the apostles in prison shortly after Christ's resurrection. The apostle Peter was in prison twice and he was miraculously freed. The stories of his imprisonment and subsequent freedom are told in Acts chapters 5 and 12. Angels came and opened the doors and Peter left. To me, a more remarkable story is the story of Paul. His prison experience is described in Acts 16, verses 23-34: "**When they had struck them with many blows, they threw them into prison, commanding the jailer to guard them securely; and he, having received such a command, threw them into the inner prison and fastened their feet in stocks. But about midnight Paul and Silas were praying and singing hymns of praise to God, and the prisoners were listening to them; and**

suddenly there came a great earthquake, so
that the foundations of the prison house were
shaken; and immediately all the doors were
opened and everyone's chains were unfastened.
When the jailer awoke and saw the the prison
doors open, he drew his sword and was about
to kill himself, supposing that the prisoners had
escaped. But Paul cried out with a loud voice,
saying 'Do not harm yourself, for we are all
here!' And he called for lights and rushed in,
and trembling with fear he fell down before
Paul and Silas, and after he brought them out,
he said, 'Sirs, what must I do to be saved?'
So they said, 'Believe in the Lord Jesus, and
you will be saved, you and your household.'
And then they spoke the word of the Lord to
him together with all who were in his house.
And he took them that very hour of the night
and washed their wound, and immediately he
was baptized, he and all his household. And
he brought them into his house and set food
before them, and rejoiced greatly, having
believed in God with his whole household.'"

I find it very encouraging that Paul was given
the opportunity to leave but remained because
he knew he still had work to do. I wonder if
I were kidnapped by the insurgents and, by
a miraculous event, was given the chance
for freedom would I stay behind so the very
testimony of my remaining would allow
someone come to new faith in Christ. That is
what Paul did. Paul remained so he could serve
this man. What he served him was the Bread of
Life.

I think about the military members, especially the guardsmen and reservists who do not have to come but do so out of a willingness to serve. At any time they could resign, but choose to stay. They have entered the confinement of a deployed base in harm's way and have purposely given up certain freedoms to risk their lives so others may see freedom and for those of us who have freedom to may remain free.

Further in Acts we read of what leads Paul on, "And now, behold, bound by the Spirit, I am on my way to Jerusalem, not knowing what will happen to me there, except that the Holy Spirit solemnly testifies to me in every city, saying that bonds and afflictions await me. But I not consider my life of any account as dear to myself, so that I may finish my course and the ministry which I received from the Lord Jesus, to testify solemnly of the gospel of the grace of God." (Acts 20:22-24)

How many of us are like Paul and are willing to set aside our personal freedom so others may have eternal life?

Soli Deo Gloria

More thought to come

APRIL 5, 2007

Days in the life:

4/3

1200: Go to lunch

1300: Go back to my trailer and take a one hour nap before a long flight

1400: Prepare for flying a nine hour flight

1450: Arrive at Life Support and pick up my night vision goggles

1500: Briefing on Intelligence and tactics with crew

1530: Call my wife before I fly. She has asked that I tell her only after I have flown and made it back safely. This time she guesses I am about to go flying. I am sorry

1545: Head out to the aircraft

1630: Take off and fly for 8 hours and 20 minutes over Baghdad. During the flight, at the 6th hour when everyone is in a zone, I suddenly hear the co-pilot say, "Pilot, did you see that?" Almost immediately I hear the pilot say, "Pilot has the aircraft." We bank quickly to the left. What was seen was some type of munition heading in our direction. Everyone is alert and wide-awake for the rest of the flight

4/4

0100: Land and keep engines running while maintenance checks out an engine that is running a little out of specifications

0110: The engines are shut down and I go back to Life Support to turn in my night vision goggles. Go to the bathroom and try to call my

183

wife and let her know I am back on the ground. Can't get through

0120: Start walking back to my trailer, about a mile and a half

0140: Arrive at my trailer and drop my stuff go to the call center and talk to the lovely wife

0200: Read my bible

0230: Defense system fires. I was awake but, if I weren't, I would have been awakened by the sound. Turn off the lights. It fires again. Go to sleep

0710: Alarm clocks wakes me from deep slumber. I shower and get dressed

0745: Head to the hospital for intensive care unit rounds in the radiology tent. Go to ICU 2 where we have the children. Four children are on ventilators, another is a baby with serious infections due to an immunodeficiency. A variety of children are on the ward

0845: Finish rounds head back to the clinic to check e-mail. Discuss politics and religion

1045: Head to the call center to call my mom and wish her a happy birthday. I couldn't get through earlier and I only have 15 minutes to catch her while it is still the 4/3 on the west coast

1130: Go to lunch

1200: Return to my trailer to take a nap before my night shift in the contingency aeromedical staging facility (CASF) where we prepare patients for air evacuation

1310: Lay down

1610: Alarm clock wakes me from a deep nap

1620: Go to fitness center, run 4 miles, do 170 sit ups and 170 push ups

1730: Take a shower and change into my flight suit

1755: Head to the clinic for a commander's call

1820: Go to dinner

1845: Head back to my trailer to pick up a few things for my night and walk to the CASF

1900: Arrive at the CASF, check e-mail and call the lovely wife and start laundry. It isn't very glamorous war stuff, but the reality is that you need to get your laundry done or you start to lose friends

1945: Start medically clearing patients for aero-medical evacuation

2030: Go back to the operations building to drop off a piece of survival "gear" that I forgot to give back after the flight

2100: Go to hospital to clear a patient who was in a car accident. I check in on the kids in the ICU plus another one in the ward

2230: Go back to the CASF and clear patients who just came in from bases scattered around Iraq. Most are non-battle injuries. Fold laundry

2300: Go back to hospital to clear more patients who just came in by helicopter

4/5

2400: Go back to the CASF and answer some more e-mails and work on this before I forget all of the places I have been. The plane will arrive in about 2 hours and is scheduled to depart around 0450. No chance of sleep until we have loaded the patients

0040: Discuss plan to load the patients with the entire CASF staff

0140: Back to the hospital to check on a patient who is supposed to go out on a plane tonight but there is a concern that he is getting worse and might need to travel with our Critical Care Air Transport Team (CCATT)

0200: Patient looked good and was resting comfortably. Back to the CASF. The plane, a C-17, will land in about 40 minutes and then, once they remove the cargo, we will load patients. While the cargo is being unloaded, the nurse will give report and I will be available in case the air-evac nurse has any questions

0340: Arrive back at CASF

0345: Go to the hospital to clear patients who just arrived by helicopter. Three patients: one young man with a gunshot wound to the leg and two others with non-battle injuries

0410: Return to CASF. Time to try to get some sleep before the 0650 alarm clock invitation to wake up

0650: One of my fellow flight docs is my alarm clock as he appears to relieve me. I am willing to admit that I am still a little tired.

0700: Off to the hospital to round on the children before I get any more sleep

0800: In the radiology tent again to look at the studies that have been performed in the last 24 hours on the patients in the ICU

0815: Go to ICU 2 to round on the children. There are five children here today: three are on ventilators, one was just taken off the ventilator and one is the two-month-old with the immunodeficiency. I will write more about the children soon

0905: Return to the CASF to grab my stuff

0935: Walk home to my trailer

0945: Get to my trailer and prepare to take a nap

1015: Turn off the lights and go to bed. "Now Lord lay me down to sleep...."

1200: Still asleep (I wake up at 1320)

My life is probably better than most of the docs here. The surgeons sleep much less than I do. In 48 hours I got around 12 hours and 5 minutes of sleep over four different sleeping periods. Within those periods there are planes, controlled detonations and alarms that often interfere with restful sleep. This is pretty typical.

I have the honor of following my calling as a Christian physician here; however, a lot of what I do day-to-day is just a duty to fulfill my calling.

More thoughts on calling vs. duty coming soon

Soli Deo Gloria

APRIL 9, 2007

Yesterday was Easter and a very emotional day for me at the worship service. There are a few reasons that I think I was more emotional than usual. The first is the number of injured children I am seeing. The second is because of a very poignant story I heard about an 18-year-old soldier and the lieutenant that tried to save him. Lastly, it is Easter and I am away from my family and not sure if I will ever see them again in this life.

Back to my thoughts about the children of war, one of the reasons I have been deployed to the base I am at is because of the increasing number of children we are caring for who have been injured. I thought specifically about what is happening to them as I was reading in

Proverbs about the seven things that God hates. Proverbs 6:17b states that one of the things that God hates is "hands that shed innocent blood". Side by side in the ICU are two children who were severely injured by an improvised explosive device combined with chlorine gas in Ramadi the other day. We have a one-year-old boy who had some glass pieces penetrate the back of his neck, but his main problem is the damage caused to his lungs from breathing chlorine gas. He has been on a ventilator for three days while we wait to see if his lungs recover. We are hopeful. The other child is a 13-year-old girl. As they were examining her in the ER the surgeon told me of how beautifully her toenails were painted and she was found to be holding a flower when she was taken to the OR. She was taken to the OR to repair the left side of her face that was just about blown off. When I first saw her in the ICU her face was still covered with some blood and there was a patch of skin sown to cover where her left eye used to be. When you looked at her right side you could tell she was a beautiful girl, carrying a flower she had picked from a field. Now she will be forever disfigured. There is absolutely no doubt that these children's bodies flow with innocent blood and the very fact that their blood was shed represents something God hates. I am wondering where Al Jazeera or CNN or BBC is to report this act of terror against children…and the loving care they are receiving from the "infidels".

Unfortunately, I am sharing about just two of a constant stream of children I see as a result of

the terrorist attacks that continue to destabilize
Iraq. That is one of the differences I see
from the last time I was here. The number of
injured U.S. military is about the same, but the
number of Iraqi civilians, especially children,
has gone up dramatically. Where is the moral
outrage? These attacks against the children
at schools and markets were not aimed at the
U.S. military and if we leave the chances are
they will only get worse. I asked my Muslim
translator one day how believers of Islam can
justify such attacks. He is a very educated man
and a devout Muslim. He explained to me why
the Quran does not approve of these types of
attacks against Muslim children. I then asked
him the percentage of Muslims in the Middle
East that felt the same way he did and he
answered, "About two percent."

As I stood and looked at these two children in
the ICU I wondered what effect this will have
on me when I return home. I am often asked
how I deal with the difficulty of caring for
severely ill children. I am able to process the
tragedy of children born with heart defects,
although there are still days I cry, much like
Jesus did when He joined in mourning for
Lazarus, even though he knew was going the
raise him from the dead (John Chapter 11). I
am also encouraged by the story of when Jesus
is asked why a child was born blind and was
it due to sin in the lives of the parents or the
child. Jesus responds, **"It was neither that this
man sinned, nor his parents; but it was so that
the works of God might be displayed in him."
(John 9:3)** It is much more difficult to handle

all of the carnage I am seeing. I think the ultimate answer is the same with the exception that man can do little to change the number of children with heart defects. However, man is directly responsible and will be held accountable for the innocent blood of these children.

What do I consider the ultimate answer? The ultimate answer I give for how I handle the suffering of children comes from five very important principles from my faith: 1) God is omniscient, omnipotent, and loving; 2) God knows the number of our days before our life begins ["Your eyes have seen my unformed substance; and in Your book were all written the days that were ordained for me, when as yet there was not one of them."(Psalm 139:16,3)]; 3) Children who die go to heaven regardless of their parents' faith or whether they have been baptized; 4) God is allowing things to continue that He hates for a period of time because of the fallen nature of man; and 5) man's intellect is too feeble to understand the permissive will of God. "Trust in the Lord with all of your heart, and do not lean on your own understanding; (Proverbs 3:5)" Because of #5 I place all of my trust in #1.

The uniting scripture I can rest on is this: "But when the perfect comes, the partial will be done away. When I was a child, I used to speak like a child, think like a child. When I became a man, I did away with childish things. For now we see in a mirror dimly, but then face to face; now, I know in part, but then I will know fully just as I also have been fully known. But now faith, hope, and love, abide these three. But the greatest of these is love."(1 Corinthians 13:10-13)

You see, as a physician, I feel God allows me to take part in His plan but not to change the ultimate plan He has for His Glory. I do not believe that I save anyone's life with my medical care. That is the business of God. I see my role as a Christian physician to direct parents and patients to give all healing credit to the Great Physician. As C. Everett Koop so elegantly stated, "I can sew two pieces of skin together but it is God who sends the fibroblasts to heal the incision."

Easter is truly the "high holiday" for Christians. Without the Easter story, Christianity is just a nice story about a man who died. With Easter we see the Creator giving his life as a sacrifice for those He created. His perfect life as a human allowed Him to conquer death for all of us and gives us hope. My faith gives me hope to trust in the love that ultimately saves me...and the children who die in war.

Soli Deo Gloria

More thoughts to come

APRIL 10, 2007

Before I left on my first tour of Iraq, I gave my wife, my mother, and my in-laws a Service Star Banner. What follows describes the Service Star Banner and is from: **www. bluestarmothers.org**

Display of the Service Star Banner first came about during World War I. During WWI and WWII most flags were hand made by mothers across the nation. One of the most famous flags was that of the five Sullivan brothers who all perished on the U.S.S. Juneau.

Each blue star on the flag represents a service member in active duty. A gold star is displayed if a service member is killed in action or dies in service. If several stars are displayed in one family the gold star takes the honor of being placed at the top. Display of a Service Star Banner is done during times of war.

When my wife found out I was returning to Iraq one of her first comments was: "I will get out the star and put it back in the window."

The star is a great reminder of the how many are affected when a service members goes off to war. To me the star is a declaration that should be acknowledged and acted upon. The support I get as a member of the armed forces is amazing. Even with all of the negative media attention, great Americans everywhere are deluging us with food, treats, clothes, toiletries, coffee and letters of encouraging thoughts and prayers. During Veterans Day and Memorial Day we are usually asked to stand for recognition. We are often acknowledged at sporting events. All of these are a great honor and very much appreciated to counteract all that is said on CNN or in most newspapers.

But what does the star mean to me? It means that my wife is a temporary widow, my son is a temporary orphan, and my parents have temporarily lost a son. Accordingly, I would ask that in following with what God has stated throughout the scriptures and most clearly in James 1:27: **"Pure and undefiled religion in the sight of our God and Father is this: to visit orphans and widows in their distress, and to keep oneself unstained by the world."**

So the next time you drive by a car or a house and you see a blue star surrounded by a red border, consider what you can do to look after these orphans and widows. If you see a gold star waving from a proudly displayed Service Banner, mourn with them.

In a letter to the Philippians, Paul writes, **"For to me, to live is Christ and die is gain. But if I am to live on in the flesh, this will mean fruitful labor for me; and I do not know which to choose. But I am hard pressed by both…"** (Philippians 1:21-23a) I put all of my **trust in** the Lord and would be honored if a banner with a gold star waved gently from our flagpole by our front door; yet pray that my star remains blue.

Soli Deo Gloria

More thoughts to come

APRIL 11, 2007

On Easter, there was incredible act of bravery
that few will hear of. There was a gun battle
that was going on and an 18-year-old member
of the infantry was shot in the shoulder. He
was wounded and pinned down. His lieutenant
saw that was one his men was trapped and
injured. The natural reaction for most would
be to run and protect yourself, being thankful
that you were not injured. However, there is
a much-honored concept in the military and
that is "We leave no man behind." It is not
always possible, but it is not just a lofty ideal.
It is considered to be part of one's duty. The
lieutenant knew his duty. This man was one of
his and, as an officer, it was his responsibility
to keep his men safe. It is also the officer's
duty to call the family if one of their men is
injured or killed. This lieutenant ran to his
injured soldier to help get him to the medevac
helicopter that was already on the way. As
he ran to his man, he was shot many times.
Now the lieutenant was much more injured
than the soldier under his charge. Now it was
the soldier's duty to get the lieutenant help.
The medevac helicopter landed and with help
from many others they were able to get the
lieutenant and his soldier on the helicopter. On
the short ride to our hospital the lieutenant's
heart stopped on the helicopter. When it landed
the medic was actively doing CPR. The rest of
the story comes from a nurse I work with that
was a witness. The first litter had the dying
lieutenant with the medic on the litter doing
CPR. The second litter off the helicopter had

the soldier who had been shot in the shoulder, blood flowing from his shoulder. They both had done their duty. The lieutenant died. The nurse cried with the chaplain as they watched this event transpire.

This event is filled with tragedy, bravery, honor, and dedication to duty. As I think about the actions of the lieutenant I am reminded about the difference between our calling and our duty. I see our calling as the purpose of our life and the duties we have are those activities that allow us to accomplish our purpose. The idea of a purpose to a life is why I think "The Purpose Driven Life" was such a popular book. People like to feel there is some purpose to their life. The lieutenant was called to serve his country, which was his purpose. He died while performing the duty of his calling. The purpose of a soldier is not to die; however, he may die while performing his duties.

I believe we all have a calling or a purpose. It is the path that God calls us to walk. Our unique "calling" has wonderful attributes of servanthood, sacrifice, charity, and generosity. Our duty is what is required to carry out our calling. I often see people who have mistakenly thought that their day-to-day duties were their calling. I believe God desires much more from us. The people who consider their duties their calling are often frustrated. I think of the stay-at-home mom, the father who works very hard to support his family and does

little else with his extra time besides bowling
and watching sports on TV, the retired couple,
or the young college student—all who may
feel unfulfilled. The matron who cares for
our orphans in Zambia (my wife and I have
a non-profit organization that supports an
orphanage in Zambia) has a calling to care for
orphans. The changing of the diapers, washing
the endless clothes or feeding the infants is
not a very glamorous duty, but what keeps it
from becoming an arduous task is that it is
associated with a calling of service.

I frequently hear of families that say that their
calling is to their family and use this as an
excuse why they cannot serve more. I would
say that our responsibility to our families is
an expected duty given to us from God. There
are many who raise their families in addition
to also serving on the mission field, feeding
homeless, or finding some other way to serve,
sacrifice, give, or comfort those in need. I
know of a couple from medical school. He is
a family practice doctor and she is a stay-at-
home mom with four children. Shortly after
finishing his residency they took their family
to Kazakstan. They have a clinic for the poor
and lead Muslim doctors to Christ, and she has
a great ministry to the local women. They are
currently being threatened for their bold faith
but remain strong and committed to their call.
Often the fear of duty keeps people from their
call and God is a gentleman. He does not force
people to follow Him, love Him, or serve Him.

I am encouraged by how many families make sending encouraging notes to soldiers a part of their family activities. In the U.S. it is easy for us to get caught up in lessons, sports, and activities with our children, but how many of those activities will bear any eternal fruit in the orchard God has given us to sow and reap from?

I have become very sensitized to how meaningless many of our activities are that take up so much of our time. How much of what we do will last past the judgment seat of Christ, into eternity? "For we must all appear before the judgment seat of Christ, so that each of may be recompensed for what his deeds in the body, according to what he has done, whether good or bad." (2 Corinthians 5:10) and "Each man's work will become evident, for the day will show it, because it is to be revealed with fire, and the fire itself will test the quality of each man's work. If any man's work which he has built on it remains, he will receive a reward. If any man's work is burned up, he will suffer loss, but he himself will be saved; yet so as through fire." (1 Corinthians 3:13-15) I wonder how much time in Christian homes was spent this Easter on coloring eggs, making baskets, hiding and finding eggs, and getting pictures with the Easter bunny. I wonder in the same homes how much time was spent talking about the true meaning of Easter besides that which was discussed in church. Jesus has called us to be servants and what that means is this: we are to be servants to others not to ourselves.

What is your calling? If your call is clear, the obstacles of your duties are to be expected and overcome by God's grace. He uses these to refine us. We are put in positions of trust where we have nowhere to turn except God. That is where He wants us. He wants our problems to be bigger than what we can solve so we can grow in our faith and find Him faithful. **"For God has not given us a spirit of fearfulness, but one of power, love, and sound judgment."** (2 Timothy 1:7) New International Version

Daily I am reminded how precious and fleeting life can be as I see how weak skin, flesh and bones are compared to the power of gunpowder. Everyday, not knowing the length of my days, I must ask myself, "Am I following my calling or just doing my duty?"

Soli Deo Gloria

More thoughts to come

APRIL 21, 2007

Yesterday, it was reported that Senate Majority leader Harry Reid stated, "... the President knows that this war is lost and the surge is not accomplishing anything as indicated by the extreme violence in Iraq yesterday".

You can imagine it depends a lot on who you talk to, but the bottom line is that it is an absolute morale killer when you have someone so high in government state your efforts are futile and the war you are fighting is a lost cause. I consider these statements treason. I also think anyone who feels you can find a middle ground and negotiate with someone who is willing to blow up innocent women and children has no idea about the ideology we are dealing with.

The war in Iraq is over and has been won. The war on terror continues. The civil war in Iraq is a product of the Islamic religion. Until we place the blame on the ideology and fight the ideology in all ways (militarily, diplomatically, socially, and psychologically), we will be frustrated with little success in our goals.

I have included a brilliant essay from a great thinker who has examined the play book on how North Viet Nam was able to defeat a much more powerful U.S. There are many lessons to be learned, as well as appreciate that we have a growing enemy to freedom in the U.S. and it comes from within.

The Fifth Column
Paul R. Hollrah

March 3, 2007

The August 3, 1995 edition of the Wall Street Journal carried an interview with former *North Vietnamese Colonel Bui Tin, a member of the North Vietnamese general staff* and the man who received the surrender of South Vietnam's President Duong Van Minh on April 30, 1975. The interview was conducted by Stephen Young, a Minnesota human rights activist.

Colonel Tin described the military and political events of the war from his vantage point in Hanoi. What *he described was the step-by-step defeat of U.S. forces, not on the battlefield, but in the White House, in the Halls of Congress, in the streets of America, and on our college and university campuses.* Sound familiar?

As I read Col Tin's recitation of how events played out in Vietnam - step-by-step-by-step - *I couldn't help but think of the motto embroidered across the shoulder patch that I wore during the last eighteen months of my military service.* The shoulder patch was the insignia of the U.S. 7th Army and the motto embroidered across the bottom read, *"Seven Steps To Hell."*

Col. Tin was asked, *"How did Hanoi intend to defeat the Americans?" He responded, "By fighting a long war which would break their will. Ho Chi Minh said, 'We don't need to win military victories, we only need to hit them until they give up and get out.' "*
(Note: I heard of a North Vietnamese officer saying, "We can go on losing longer than you (America) can go on winning." - Norm)

Liberals, cut-and-run Democrats and the anti-war left now signal to al Qaeda and Islamic Jihad that we're preparing to do the same in Iraq.

Step One.

Col Tin was asked, *"Was the American anti-war movement important to Hanoi's victory?" He responded, "It was essential to our strategy.* Every day our leadership would listen to world news over the radio at 9:00 AM to follow the growth of the American anti-war movement.

Visits to Hanoi by people like Jane Fonda and former Attorney General Ramsey Clark...gave us confidence that we should hold on in the face of battlefield reverses."

Jane Fonda and Ramsey Clark are back, and they've been joined by Cindy Sheehan, a host of anti-war leftists, and nearly the entire Democrat Party, all bashing the Commander in Chief and clamoring for an early surrender in Iraq.

Step Two.

Col. Tin was asked, *"How could the Americans have won the war?"* He responded, *"Cut the Ho Chi Minh trail inside Laos. If Johnson had granted (General) Westmoreland's requests to enter Laos and block the Ho Chi Minh trail, Hanoi could not have won the war."*

While George W. Bush has given battlefield commanders all of the troops and equipment they've requested, Democrats complain that it's either too little or too much.

Step Three.

Col. Tin was asked, *"What of American bombing of North Vietnam?"* He responded, "If all the bombing had been concentrated at one time, it would have hurt our efforts. But *the bombing was expanded in slow stages under Johnson and it didn't worry us."*
In the Iraq War, Rules of Engagement are written by lawyers in the Pentagon.
(Note: I have said before that lawyers shouldn't be allowed inside Barrett range of a military decision. The

*job of a lawyer is generally either to look for reasons
something CAN'T be done or to confuse the issues- Norm)*

Step Four.

Col. Tin was asked, "What about Westmoreland's
strategy and tactics caused you concern?" He responded,
"Our senior commander in the South, Gen. Nguyen Chi
Thanh, knew that *we were losing base areas, control of
the rural population, and that his main forces were being
pushed out to the borders of South Vietnam. Johnson had
rejected Westmoreland's request for 200,000 more troops
(and) we realized that America had made its maximum
military commitment to the war.* "

*Democrats and anti-war radicals maintain constant
pressure to turn public opinion against the administrations
new "troop surge" strategy, even threatening to cut off
funding for our troops.*

Step Five.

Col. Tin continued, "*Tet was designed to influence
American public opinion.* We would attack poorly defended
parts of South Vietnam cities during a holiday. when few
South Vietnamese troops would be on duty. *Our losses
were staggering. (General) Giap later told me that Tet had
been a military defeat, though we had gained the planned
political advantages when Johnson agreed to negotiate* and
did not run for reelection."

*In America, in 2006, Democrats and anti-war radicals
hounded a highly competent Defense Secretary out of
office and used bloated anti-war rhetoric to gain victories
in the mid-term elections.*

Step Six.

Col. Tin was asked, *"What of Nixon?"* He responded,
"Well, *when Nixon stepped down because of Watergate we knew we would win.* (Prime Minister) Pham Van Dong said of Gerald Ford. 'He's the weakest president in US history; the people didn't elect him. Even if you gave him candy he doesn't dare intervene in Vietnam again.' "

So who will Islamic Jihad see across the battle lines in the next administration. Hillary Clinton? Barack Hussein Obama? A trial lawyer from North Carolina?

Step Seven.

"Seven Steps To Hell", *and one day Democrats will be called to answer for each and every one of them.*
Paul R. Hollrah is a senior fellow at the Lincoln Heritage Institute.

No one should consider that telling a soldier, who has lost a buddy, been injured, or spent months away from home, that bringing him home and calling the war he was fighting lost by the U.S. is by any means supporting him. The morale of the troops is decreasing and I think it is due mostly to a constant barrage of being told we are losing. "I support the troops. Bring them home now" bumper stickers show the great ignorance of those who have never been at war. Pride, honor and satisfaction come from finishing the job you were sent to do and knowing that the fans in the stands really want you to win and will stay in the cold, wind, snow, sleet and rain until the very end.

Soli Deo Gloria

More thoughts to come

APRIL 22, 2007

Caring for the wounded and sick children of war, I have many opportunities to see the families who are devastated by how their child has been drawn into this conflict of men. In war there are times when children are innocently harmed when a bomb or a bullet goes astray or when children are being housed with terrorists. Unfortunately, what is becoming more common here is the purposeful targeting of areas that are known to have children present e.g., markets and streets near schools. It is hard to understand the mind of the person who would purposely target the innocent. It seems like these acts are done without demands of money or power. We are somewhat used to groups taking credit for acts of terrorism with demands of money, release of someone or statement against a government by blowing up a specific building; however, it seems like such demands have become rare when a suicide bomber explodes in the middle of a fruit stand. It is easy to lose track of the religious motivation for who is getting blown up. Some days we get wounded children from a Sunni neighborhood and others times they are from a Shiite neighborhood. It should be noted that many families are mixed, with the wife a Sunni and the husband a Shiite, and vice versa. They are able to live in peace and often express confusion about the violence in their own country. The attacks appear to be vengeful explosions against those who require no vengeance. For the thoughtful person the answer to the obvious question of "Why?" seems to be lacking. I was struggling with the question and had just assumed it was part of living in a fallen world. That was until I came across the following verse in Isaiah.

"Behold I am going to stir up the Medes against them, who will not value silver or take pleasure in gold. And their bows will mow down young men. They will not even have compassion on the fruit of the womb. Nor will their eye pity children." (Isaiah 13:17-18)

The "them" that I underlined is referring to Babylon, which happens to be in Iraq. Medes is considered to be ancient Iran. I am not sure that this verse is specifically dealing with today's events but it sure rings true. Now, to be fair to the verse, ancient Iran and Iraq have waged many wars against each other. One should also remember that the majority of the current borders were only recently drawn during the early 1900's so what we think of Iraq and Iran may be much different than it was when Isaiah wrote such powerful words. Regardless it is a verse that is true today.

When I was in Yemen a couple of months ago there was a civil war going on. The war was in the North. My Yemeni interpreter was a devout

Muslim and quick to say that he disagreed with President Bush on just about everything except one thing. I asked him what the civil war was about. He was exasperated as he explained that it was a conflict caused by Iran because they wanted to bring about a Shiite stronghold in the North. He went on to state that the Iranian agents had already forced out all of the Jews that had been peacefully living there for thousands of years. The Yemeni merchants consider the Jews to be the most skilled craftsman and silversmiths; they make what are considered to be the best swords that are proudly worn on the belts of the Yemeni men. The one thing he agreed with President Bush about was this: The U.S. must not leave until Iraq is stable or Iran will try to take over all of Arabia.

The good news is that in the midst of all of the conflict all around the world the Creator of the universe is still on the throne and is ultimately in charge. What is happening here is no surprise to Him. **"For by Him all things were created, both in the heavens and on earth, visible and invisible, whether thrones or dominions or rulers or authorities—all things have been created through Him and for Him."** (Colossians 1:16) For some this verse may be confusing and may not seem like good news at all. The key is knowing the end of the story. We have been given the end of the story. It is found in Revelation chapters 19, 20, and 21. Read the book.

Soli Deo Gloria

More thoughts to come

APRIL 28, 2007

Can you catch a mosquito with your toes?

It is an interesting time of year and, for those that enjoy sports, it is a truly special time. The NFL draft, NBA and NHL playoffs, and the start of Major League Baseball all are going on right now. As I was walking to my assigned duty this morning I was thinking about what makes people special. What makes people admire someone? There is much to admire as I care for very brave men and women here, but what is it that I specifically admire? What sets someone apart?

I remember when I was a boy of about nine years my dad had a friend who was a black belt in Karate. The story goes that he could catch a mosquito between his first and second toe. I don't think this was true, but I believed it. This amazed me and I shared this story with my grandmother. She was not impressed and wanted me to be more impressed with my own father and how he had handled losing most of his left arm. I thought she was way off. My dad had just lost something; his friend Mike could do something that was very cool!!

That interaction has stayed with me for over 30 years. While I continued my half-mile walk to the place where the wounded wait for the next flight (CASF) , I thought about how the type of people I admire has changed with time. When I was a boy, before I became a Christian, I admired people who could catch mosquitoes

in unique ways. I would also admire great
athletes, television stars, or people who could
easily get girls to like them (that was never my
gift). When I became a Christian, I began to
change who I admired. Now it was the pastor
of a very large church who had written books,
the Christian music star etc. From the Bible
I knew they were just like me but I wanted
to meet them, have them know me, and have
them sign something for me. As I got a chance
to spend a little more time with some of the
"big name" pastors of California, I became
convinced that they were much more like
me than they were like God. This is to take
nothing away from them or to elevate myself,
but just an awareness of the mightiness of God.
Now there are some people who hardly anyone
in the world may notice who I admire greatly
and there are those that are well known that
I do not admire at all. What has changed? As
I thought of how I would put into words my
feeling toward the admiration of man, this is
what I came up with: I admire people based
on how much they allow God to accomplish
things through them. These people are not
walking advertisements for themselves.
They do not talk about "their" ministry; they
call it God's. They do not talk of "their"
accomplishments; they use every opportunity
to bring glory to God for what He has done.
They are walking billboards to the strength and
power of a life totally dedicated to and truly
transformed by God.

It is easy to see how we are becoming a society
that worships men and women, be they pastors,

scientists, athletes, musicians or movie stars.
John Wesley said, "Give me twelve men who
love Jesus with all their hearts and who do
not fear men or devils, and I care not one whit
whether they be clergy or laity. With these men
I will change the world."

I will probably never be a national hero, a rock
star, or a NBA Hall of Famer, but I could be
one of those men John Wesley described. The
question I must ask myself is, "am I willing"?

Soli Deo Gloria

More thoughts to come

MAY 7, 2007

I wonder how many people become concerned
when the phone rings. I wonder how many
people are suddenly worried when they see an
official vehicle drive into their neighborhood.
I wonder how many parents only get to speak
to their spouse 15 minutes twice a week to
discuss all of the household issues and how to
deal with rebellious children. I wonder how
many people wonder if their loved one is OK
if the phone disconnects. I wonder. This is
the life of the family of a serviceman who is
deployed in harm's way.

The other night we had the Wing
Commander's Call for officers. This was
to recognize our achievements during this
rotation. As we were in our seats waiting for
the room to be called to attention, my friend,
who is an orthopedic surgeon, sat down beside

me and explained that it was a bad day as some of our men had died in an IED explosion. As we were discussing all of the medical issues, the room was called to attention. General Rand started his comments with the history of the 332 Air Expeditionary Wing. Those who serve in the 332 are known as Tuskegee Airman because it started as the Wing for the now famous black pilots. He went on to explain the recent honor the few remaining pilots received from President Bush. In recognition for their heroic efforts during WWII they were given the Congressional Gold Medal. After finishing his remarks President Bush saluted the airmen, saying he wanted to offer the gesture to "help atone for all the unreturned salutes and unforgivable indignities" they endured. President Bush then went on to say that we as a country were indebted to these men. One of the pilots responded that with this award the debt was paid in full. The General took quite some time explaining all that these pilots had accomplished and how "they had to fight for the right to fight". I feel indebted to these men for the doors they forced open for my son. General Rand then spent time speaking of the many achievements that were accomplished during our almost four months here. He thanked us for all we had done.

Next he paused and his voice quivered a bit. He then asked how many of us had spouses. About half of the room raised their hands and I could feel tears welling up. He explained that he felt that it is harder on the spouse than for the one deployed. They are the ones who have to keep the house and the children together while we are gone. They wait by the phones, struggle with the children, and have to manage everything. He wondered how hard it must be to watch CNN when your loved one is in harm's way. He then said, "Please tell your spouses, I thank them for all they have sacrificed for you to serve here." He then asked how many have children and a few less people raised their hands. The General said, "Please thank your sons and daughters for all they have done without by having you here." Deployments are hard on children and my family has not escaped the pain. Imagine a child lacking the security of whether a parent will ever come home. They live with a parent who struggles to keep it all together and watches them as they cry from sadness, fear or frustration. He then asked how many still had parents living and most raised their hands. My mom is overjoyed when I call and sends me cards and care packages frequently. I am quite confident that she has prayed more for me than I have prayed for her or myself. He said, "I think it is hardest on the mothers to have their sons and daughters at war. Please thank your parents for me." He then asked how many were grandparents and a few raised their hands. What he stated next rang true for all of us in the large tent. He stated what we are doing today has a direct impact on the life of the grandchildren represented in the room. Joseph Lieberman wrote a very articulate op. ed. piece recently discussing that Al-Queda has left us with one choice and that is to stay and stabilize the region from the terrorists. I would encourage everyone to read the short article. It can be found in the April 26, 2007 edition of The Washington Post.

The General explained that only 20% of the Air Force has been deployed to Iraq and thanked us again and reminded us of the honor of being a Tuskegee Airman. Over the past two years I have spent 8 months in Iraq. I thank all of my family for being such a wonderful support and, on behalf of General Robin Rand, thank you. You have served me valiantly.

It is a true honor and with great pride that I can call myself a Tuskegee Airman.

Soli Deo Gloria

More thoughts to come

MAY 7, 2007

Moments that Matter:

I have witnessed a couple of spontaneous events recently that have really moved me and I wanted to share them.

The first event that I want to describe occurred last night before we started watching Spiderman 3 at the base theater. Before each picture that is shown a giant "Please Rise" comes up on the screen. Everyone in the theater dutifully rises for the National Anthem. The military is a pretty patriotic group and so the National Anthem plays as we all stand at attention, as this is the standard. I have noticed at ballparks and other venues where the National Anthem is played that often hats are not removed and many people will continue to talk through the song, but not here. About halfway through the National Anthem, the film broke and the sound and background went off. The fully packed theater stood in silence, at attention, and no one moved. One could have heard a pin drop as we all were waiting for the completion of the song we hold so dear. A few moments later, the National Anthem and the background film started again from the beginning and stopped in the same place. There was about a five second pause and then a solitary voice was heard and then hundreds joined in as the theater finished the Star Spangled Banner accapela. When we finished singing, thunderous applause rose from the theater. It was in stark contrast to what usually happens as we usually stand at attention in silence and then sit down without a word. This night was special and all the people in the theater knew it.

The next event occurred a couple of weeks ago while we were loading a plane full of injured servicemen on their way to Germany. The plane was a C-17, which is a new huge cargo plane. It is well lit and is an absolute joy to work and fly on. It is especially nice to transport patients on. The only drawback about this plane is that it only carries enough litter stanchions to hold nine litter patients. To allow us to carry more than nine patients, the plane carries a very large green that holds additional litter stanchions. This box is about a 9-foot cube and has a big red cross painted on the end that points to the rear of the aircraft and is positioned all the way in the rear of the aircraft. On this day, there was a three by five foot flag proudly displayed over the red cross. People are familiar with military members saluting the flag as it passes them in formation or standing when it passes in a parade. There is great reverence given to this symbol of our nation and freedom, just like the singing or playing of the National Anthem.

We were about half way done loading the plane and I was helping carry an Army Sergeant Major, the highest-ranking enlisted service member in the Army, onto the plane. We carry people onto the plane feet first and most just lie back, close their eyes and hope we don't drop them. In my personal experience of eight months of doing this I haven't heard that we have dropped one yet. Four people usually carry a litter unless it is very heavy and then there will be six. Today three others and I were carrying this soldier on and we had to pass by the giant green box with the flag facing him. His eyes were not closed and, as we passed the flag and in what seemed to be an entirely natural gesture, this injured soldier saluted the flag as he passed while lying on the litter. It is the only time I had ever seen it done and it brought tears to my eyes. As we loaded the Sergeant Major on the stanchion, I reached down and patted this soldier and thanked him for his salute. This man even though injured, never lost his military bearing. What an example. I would guess that he was saddened

by having to leave the fight—most soldiers like
him are—but I bet he was glad he was saluting
the flag rather than being draped by it.

Soli Deo Gloria

More thoughts to come

MAY 16, 2007

Deployment vs. Pregnancy:

Deployment could be likened to a pregnancy.
Before a woman gets pregnant she is often
excited to become pregnant and anxiously
awaits the positive test. Before a deployment,
service members anxiously await getting
to their destination so they can serve. Once
the initial joy of pregnancy is over then the
drudgery sets in: the bloating, the difficulty
sleeping, too many trips to the bathroom,
cravings etc. In a deployment the initial
excitement and novelty usually wears off
pretty quickly as well. There is difficulty
sleeping, new food, new beds, walking to
showers, alarm reds, wearing heavy protective
gear even to the bathroom and cravings of
food from home. As the expected time of birth
approaches, sleep is difficult, bathroom trips
are frequent, legs become numb from just
lying on one's back and expressions like "I
wish I would just have this baby already; I am
ready to stop being pregnant." can be heard.
As we near then end of our deployment, we are
constantly asking what is the news about our
replacements, when are they arriving, when
are we leaving etc. We wonder if we might be

one of those stories where the person who is leaving in a week, day or hour gets injured or, worse yet, killed just before they would have gone home. We are ready to be done being deployed. Just as a pregnant mother longs to hold their new baby, we long to hold our loved ones. Then the birth occurs and through much pain, screaming, crying, and statements of "never again," a baby makes it through a passage that few would have ever thought could have passed a baby's shoulders. The baby is now in the mother's arms and carried out of the hospital. As days and weeks pass and she receives the first smile from her precious gift, the memory of the pain and frequent trips to the bathroom starts to fade and the thought of having another baby may be considered.

This being my second deployment, I have relived many of the tragedies, hurts, and annoyances that had faded from my memory after my first time here. The joy I have now is the anticipation of seeing my wife, son, family and friends. What I carry home from the hospital is the honor of having the privilege of taking care of very brave armed service members and innocent Iraqi children. I also carry some of the most horrible images of war one could imagine, which may hide in the corners of my mind, but will probably never leave.

There is a beautiful verse in 1 Peter that applies to all trials and difficult situations and it has encouraged me through many dark times:

"After you have suffered for a little while, the God of all grace, who called you to His eternal glory in Christ, will Himself perfect, confirm, strengthen, and establish you." (1 Peter 5:10)

Soli Deo Gloria

More thoughts to come

MAY 17, 2007

Casualties of War:

Women and children are both a direct and indirect casualty of war. One of my roles during this deployment has been to care for the children who have been injured, as well as care for those who have come to our gates seeking help. Many Iraqis consider our base the only place in their country where their children can be helped.

There are many reasons why children are injured. The most common reason children come to us is from IED blasts or mortar attacks. The terrorists have increasingly targeted civilians in places where many children can be found. The next way children are injured is by bullets or bombs intended for the terrorists. To avoid being captured, the terrorists often set up their mini-bases in apartment complexes, schools, or mosques. They will then fire rockets or other weapons at soldiers who are passing by and the soldiers will return fire with machine guns, rockets, or missiles. Unfortunately, since the terrorists use women and children as their human shields, there will be times when the innocent will be harmed or killed inadvertently. The coalition forces have done everything possible to avoid harming civilians, even causing an increase in risk to all of the ground troops. This is what separates us from the barbarous acts of the terrorist. No American soldier would ever think of hiding behind a woman or child; the terrorists due this commonly.

Taking care of the children has been both a blessing and a hardship. I love to be able to help the innocents recover; however, seeing the daily carnage involving children has taken its emotional toll on me.

There are a number of children who stand out in my memory. One such young lady was 11 years old. She came to us with a badly fractured thigh bone. She had been shot in the leg and required extensive surgery, and will need more in the future, to replace a 4-inch segment of bone that is now missing. She had a face that could brighten the entire ICU. As she woke from anesthesia and began to recover, her face became even more radiant with an unexplainable joy. She enjoyed playing and coloring with the staff and the war weary staff would gravitate to her. It was only later as we were trying to find out about living family members that the other side of the story came out. She had been shot by Americans. She described how she was riding in the back of her car and her father and mother were in the front of the car. They were at a checkpoint and all of a sudden gunfire started. The next thing she knew was the pain of having been shot. Her mother and father lay dead in the front seat. The exact interaction is not clear but rockets and IEDs were found in the back of their car and then bullets started flying. A man came to visit her after about a week. He said he was a relative, but she stated that she did not know him. The agents in charge of such visits became suspicious and followed the man and he was also found to be an insurgent and was arrested. When we heard the story we were amazed at her countenance considering she was being cared for by the exact same military that had killed her parents. I hope it was because she could sense she was being lovingly cared for. This is a relatively nice story. There are many others where the children have had horrible brain injuries from which they will never recover.

It is a couple of weeks before I am scheduled to leave. I have become desensitized to brutally injured children. My eyes have dried. My heart lacks the ache these children used to cause. When I have lost the moral outrage over the "Children of War" it is time for a break to regain my perspective.

Soli Deo Gloria

One final thought to come

MAY 18, 2007

Final thought

I am flying on a C-17 to Andrews AFB. I have
finished my second tour in Iraq and now I am
accompanying about 40 injured soldiers home.
I am on this flight as a medical attendant for an
Army sergeant who was shot in the back by the
Taliban after leaving a "peace talk" meeting
the U.S. Army had set up to help the Afghani
and Pakistani border guards get along. As he
and his fellow soldiers left the meeting, they
were ambushed by members of the Taliban
from behind. He was shot in the back three
times. He requires an attendant so continuous
pain medicine can be slowly dripped directly
over his spinal nerves (an epidural) for pain
relief. It is an honor to leave my deployment in
Iraq in this manner.

I am excited to be on my way home but it
has not been certain that I would be leaving
on time. I was originally schedule to be at
a different base, but was changed at the last
minute so my skills in pediatric critical care
could be used to treat the growing number of
Iraqi children who are being cared for at the
Air Force Theater Hospital due to the increased
targeting of civilians. In fact, there are reports
that children are sometimes deliberately shot
by the terrorists because an injured child will
definitely bring the U.S. military out in the
open to rescue the child. Since I was changed
at the last moment, my orders were not
changed; thus the giant system in the sky that

controls how and when service members leave
Iraq thought I was somewhere else and had me
leaving at a much later date, even after all of
my duties at Balad were finished.

There is a reason I am getting home on time:
the prayers of the righteous. In James it states,
**"The effective prayer of a righteous man can
accomplish much."** (James 5:16b) **When it
looked like I was going to be delayed, the
wife that God has so blessed** me with called
our righteous friends and family to a time of
prayer. There were days when I could sense
God's encouragement. There were also days
when I was discouraged. I was in the midst
of birth pangs and I wanted them to be over. I
knew in my heart that God would accomplish
His perfect will and I really hoped it included
me coming home on time. After weeks of
waiting, I received my answer 12 hours before
I would leave the country. God miraculously
put it on people's hearts and minds to allow
me to leave. The details are very complicated,
but the final reason that I am on this plane
on this day is because of an Iraqi child who
continues to need our help and needed a blood
sample hand carried to Germany. The reason
I felt I so desperately needed to be home is
another chapter of my life that is still being
written and may be shared at a later date. Some
may remember from my last tour, I had a very
similar situation occur and God interceded at
the last moment to bring me home. God has
taken me through the same situation twice.
I am afraid I am not learning a lesson He is
trying to teach this very slow learner.

A man of my age who is directly across from
me at my eye level is on a litter and is going
home as well but he has lost a leg. Words are
inadequate to express my thankfulness to my
heavenly Father for getting me home...whole.

I have once again seen the absolute best and
worst of what man can do. I leave Iraq for
the second time changed and with scars few
will ever see, but it is still well my soul. This
following song has kept me glad in the midst
of trials for 26 years:

In these days of confused situations
In these nights of a restless remorse
When the heart and soul of a nation
Lay wounded and cold as a corpse
From the grave of the innocent Adam
Comes a song bringing joy to the sad
Oh your cry has been heard and the ransom
Has been paid up in full
Be Ye Glad

Now from your dungeon a rumor is stirring
You have heard it again and again
But this time the cell keys there turning
And outside there are faces of friends
And though your body lay weary from wasting
And your eyes show the sorrow they have had
All the love that your heart is now tasting
Has opened the gates
Be Ye Glad

So be like lights on the rim of the water
Giving hope in a storm sea of night
Be the refuge amidst the slaughter

Of these fugitives in their flight
For you are timeless and part of a puzzle
You are winsome and young as a lad
And there is no disease or no struggle
That can pull you from God
Be Ye Glad

Every debt that you ever had
Has been paid up in full by the grace of the
Lord

Be Ye Glad, Be Ye Glad, Be Ye Glad

BE YE GLAD

Soli Deo Gloria

NOTES

Stars and Stripes, Washington DC

The Fifth Column Paul R. Hollrah. March 3, 2007.

Koop: The memoirs of a family doctor. C. Everett Koop. Harper Collins 1993

C.T. Studd: Cricketer and Pioneer, Norman Grubb, Lutterworth Publishing, 1973

Songs:
Be Ye Glad: Michael K. Blanchard
Knowing you Jesus: Robin Mark

Movies discussed:
Gladiator 2000,
Blackhawk Down 2001,
The Patriot 2000,
The Passion 2004,
Saving Private Ryan 1998,
300 2007,
Braveheart 1995,
The Green Berets 1968,
We Were Soldiers 2002